DATE DUE	
OCT 0 1 198?	SEP 15 '98		
JAN 3 0	NOV 20 '04		
AUG 2 8 1990			
AUG 2 4 1993			
NOV 28 '94	7-19-06		
OCT 16 '95			
FEB 08 '96			
MAY 08 '96			
OCT 31 '96			
FEB 03 '97			
OCT 09 '97			

636.1 GRE

Green, Ben K.

Horse conformation as to
soundness and performance

Horse Conformation

Ben K. Green

HORSE
CONFORMATION
as to soundness and performance

NORTHLAND PRESS

Contents

Preface

THE PRIMARY PURPOSE OF THIS BOOK is to emphasize and illustrate the horse as an animal of living, mechanical perfection. The principles of mechanics, leverage and the natural law of physics were not invented by man, and were not first brought to civilization in the form of steel and other metals formed into man-made contraptions.

The first fluid shock absorber ever discovered by man had been in existence many thousands of years, that being the knee joint of a horse. The bones of the knee joint prevent the arm bone and cannon bone from coming in contact with each other. These articulating bones, which form the knee joint, are housed in a cartilage gasket and are floating in a lubricating fluid. The shock absorbers and muscular suspension of the fore part of a horse are far superior to anything that man has invented; the shoulders of a horse have no fixed bone attachment to the body and the body is suspended between the shoulders by spring-like supple muscular attachments. It is far superior to any mechanical suspension that man has thought of and has tried to imitate by the use of rubber and springs. The leverage and drive from the hindquarters, which are directly attached to the spine by the pelvis, is a far more perfect union of power for forward propulsion than any of our transmissions, universal joints, etc.

The mechanical genius of this and future generations could learn much from the mechanism of a horse and his ability to produce power and speed.

This book has been written with a performance horse in mind

that is intended for useful purposes. The subject of bone structure is discussed as to its good and bad conformation and I have endeavored to show that ideal conformation is essential to soundness and performance ability.

Technical terms and highly technical subjects have been omitted, in order that this book can be of practical value to all readers.

Heads

THE FIRST PURPOSE OF A HORSE'S HEAD, so far as the horse is concerned, is to give him balance by acting as a pendulum to help control the swinging of his body in motion. A big head on a long, weak neck does not afford a horse a desirable pendulum for balance; neither does a little light head on a heavily muscled, short neck do anything for a horse's balance.

The horse has the heaviest head in proportion to the length of his neck of any animal in the world and an ideal head on the average horse weighs about forty pounds. With the proper length of neck the use of this forty pounds can add greatly to the horse's ability to use his body and control the movement of his legs. When a horse is injured in a foreleg, he limps and lifts his body by lifting his head upward and pulling the opposite direction from the injured foreleg; if he has an injured backleg he aids the control of balance and the lifting of his body by lowering his head and pulling the opposite direction from the injured backleg. This is the most easily understood illustration of a horse's constant use of his head to give balance to the movement of his legs and body.

A horse with a head too big for his body seldom is light enough headed to be good in performance activities; a horse with an extremely light head quite often has a light mouth and is inclined to bounce and keep his front feet off the ground to the extent of creating a great deal of lost motion in movement. Extremely small heads on foals and yearlings can generally be thought of as an indication that they will lack growth factor and will mature too early without enough size and conformation. Heads on grown

I

draft horses are seldom too big and generally the collar worn by a draft horse can be slipped over his head without unbuckling.

Another most important function that the head performs is enabling the horse to breathe. The opening of the nostrils should be very wide and the walls of the nostrils should be thin and elastic with the ability to expand to take in an abundance of air. The inner nostril should not be too small since it is the chamber that tempers the air before it is drawn into contact with the lungs. This tempering of air reduces the horse's susceptibility to pneumonia, colds and other respiratory diseases. The large nostril also is essential in the exhaling of air. An extremely small outside opening of the nostril will cause the horse under stress (at running, jumping, etc.) difficulty in trying to exhale air. It will bellow up in the inner nostril and cause the horse to choke.

Since the horse's survival depends on his ability to eat and drink, the mouth, teeth, lips and tongue should be the next consideration. The teeth should be well meshed, upper and lower, and extremely hard and sound in order for the horse to be able to forage and grind food substances in a process of mastication. The ability of the horse's mouth and teeth to properly process his food has an all-important influence on his ability to digest his food substances. Good lips on a horse are essential in enabling the horse to pick up food and also in his selection and refusal of what goes into his mouth. Since the horse cannot see the end of his nose and must feel for the ground and must feel for water or his feed trough, the long hairs on the lower lips and jaw are highly essential and should never be trimmed.

Next in importance we will consider the horse's eyes. Large, dark colored eyes, wide apart and set well to the outside of the head, are essential to his good vision. The upper eyelids of a horse have the eyelashes mounted in tufts, which are dense, and prevent sweat, dust, etc. from entering the eyes from an upper angle. The lower eyelashes are usually thinner but longer to prevent objects from sweeping up into the eye. A horse has a pink third eyelid installed in the inside corner of the eye that works on the principle of a windshield wiper. When some object lands on the eyeball, the

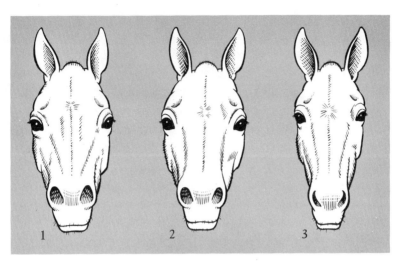

Excellent head.	*This head lacks "eye appeal" but is a good head.*	*"Cute" little worthless head.*

eyeball recedes slightly and the third eyelid flashes across the eyeball and wipes it off. The depression in the skull above the eye is of significance and aids in protecting the eye from serious injury in the event of concussion. A severe lick on the eyeball may often be sustained by the horse without severe injury to the eye because the cushion of fat behind the eye recedes up into the hollow above the eye thereby causing a shock absorption action which creates a vacuum sort of protection to the eyeball and affords the eyeball a recess that enables it to escape injury.

Good ears are neatly set just below the level of the horse's poll at the top of the head and well above the eyes. The most important point of a good ear is for it to be firmly fixed in a position that can be rotated to the furthest point backward and forward in order to bring in all elements of sound from the greatest possible area. Good, sharp, active ears are the sign of alertness, intelligence and interest in what is happening around the horse.

The overall appearance of the head is greatly enhanced by a broad, flat forehead and a nicely chisled nose together with properly set ears, eyes set well out in the side of the head, good nostrils and a well-tapered muzzle as Illustration 1 shows. A broad, flat forehead is an indication of a roomy cranial capacity set deep into the skull between the bases of the ears. The sinuses, tear ducts and breathing canals are also housed beneath this skull structure and the roomier and more properly constructed it is the better the functions can be accomplished for the welfare of the horse. It is also well known that the width of head contributes to a roomy throat-latch which is essential to breathing and the circulation purposes of the jugular vein. The distance, from a sideview, from the base of the ear to the outside corner of the eye is a determining factor in the size of the brain cavity and it is good to have the eye set a good distance below the ear. The poll between the ears needs to be extended well upward and of a very defined prominence when examined by the hand or when the foretop is pulled back from over it. This is another contribution to the size of the brain cavity and is also important to the transfer of sounds by the inner ear.

The underjaws of a horse should be somewhat flared from the inside in order to provide space for the movement of the tongue and esophagus in the process of breathing and swallowing.

The head shown in Illustration 1 would often be referred to as a *good* head but seldom would it be regarded as a *beautiful* head or a *cute* head. Because of its utility, balance and conformation, few people would recognize its fitness to serve all the purposes of a horse and man. This head would be of the greatest utility importance to the horse and his usefulness to man in that it would be capable of all the functions required of an excellent head and would afford an abundance of room for the brain cavity. This head will be in due proportion to the horse's body and will be pleasing in appearance to the human eye.

In Illustration 2 you see a head with all the necessary equipment to serve the horse and to serve mankind. However, this head is not neatly chiseled and there is apparently an excess amount of bone from the base of the eye to the end of the nose. This head lacks refinement and *eye appeal,* but it serves all the useful purposes the excellent head in Illustration 1 does.

In Illustration 3 we have a *cute, beautiful, worthless* head. This head is too light for the horse's body, will not give balance, has too

4

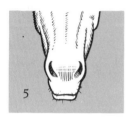

Good nostril.

Poor nostril.

Dotted line shows heavy "platter jaw."

small a brain cavity, lacks strength in the bone structure of the nose and face and is equipped with a poor set of little, narrow, inadequate nostrils. This type of head may appeal to the human eye but the horse wearing it is of little useful value. In order to have obtained this *beautiful little inadequate cranial adornment,* the horsemen must have sacrificed substance in the bone structure of the legs and have also lost much of the pendulum balance in the maneuverability of the horse's body. The breeding of such heads at the expense of the other necessities of a good horse will fast put horsemen afoot.

A heavy platter jaw on a horse, as seen in Illustration 6, is a severe fault. It may give a head the appearance of being short but it greatly adds weight to the head and because of its size it reduces the horse's ability to flex his poll and bring his neck into a good working position. The beefiness and grossness of a *platter* jaw will interfere with the breathing of a horse in action. This type of jaw usually unseats the better position of a tongue and causes the horse to have more difficulty in swallowing food and water.

In judging horses, look for heads in proportion to the horse's body, properly equipped to be of the greatest possible service to the horse and to man. Don't be misled by the *eye appeal* of a *cute* head.

5

Vision

VERY LITTLE HAS BEEN SAID OR WRITTEN concerning the eye-sight of horses. You quite often hear the common remarks, "he's pig-eyed," "wall-eyed," or that "he has a very expressive eye" or "sullen-eye" and the age-old suspicion that "a horse with white in his eye is a mean horse" which is not necessarily true. Very little has been done about the visionary deficiencies of horses.

The general description of a good eye will read, in most any text where you find the subject discussed, as "being large, round, dark in color and set well out on the side of the horse's head with great width between the eyes." Those writers who are more descriptive will go into "the eye should have a kind appearance"; "the eye should show a docile disposition"; "the eye should be active and lend beauty to the appearance of the head," etc.

All of these statements are general and are of little importance as to the actual usefulness of the horse. The perfection or imper-fection of a horse's vision greatly affects his usefulness to mankind and consequently his monetary value. We well know that injuries causing growths, blind spots and even the loss of an eye are easily detected and are not necessarily a subject of technical importance. The true vision of a horse's eye can be accurately evaluated if care-ful study is given to the color, position of the eyeball in relation to the rest of the face and the angle that the retina extends outward into the space to be viewed by the horse.

The vision of a horse is in a circular pattern, each eye having a separate circle of vision, these two circles being set at an angle comparable to the position of the eyeball in the skull. This means that the circles would barely meet at a point in front of the horse as shown in Illustration 7 and only when a horse squints his eyes can he actually see what is directly in front of him. This squinting will enable the horse to see forty to fifty feet in front of him, but the width of his muzzle causes the ability of vision by squinting to be eliminated as near as four feet and not more than six feet beyond his forehead. As he approaches an object he must turn the

6

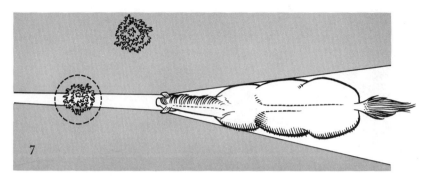

This illustration shows the pattern of vision of a horse traveling with his head and neck straight with his body. The white part is the region that the horse cannot see. The object directly in front of him with the dotted circle around it could only be seen by squinting his eyes or changing the position of his head. This illustration shows why a horse often travels with his head slightly to one side or the other.

end of his nose or his entire head slightly in order to focus one eye on the object that he originally squinted both eyes to observe.

The respective circles of vision are patterned in keeping with the angle of the "set" of the eyeball in the skull and since these two circles barely meet in front of the horse they are by necessity far wider at the back of the horse's body and in order that the horse be able to see directly behind him he must move his head to one side to the angle necessary for the "set" of his eye to be parallel to the position of the point of his hindquarter, as shown in Illustration 8. This brings into view the region from the hip bone to a distance of forty to fifty feet beyond the hindquarters.

In order to intelligently discuss the vision of a horse and the reactions that are reflected in his behavior because of his vision, we must take into account the fact that a horse may be traveling with his head and neck straight and be taking a picture on one side of a herd of cattle and on the other side he may be picturing a windmill or some other objects such as livestock, children playing, etc. His brain is so constructed that these separate pictures are clear and understandable to him. It is also true that a horse cannot see a great distance and the use of his ears enables him to bring in sound before the origin of the sound has come into his view. This ex-

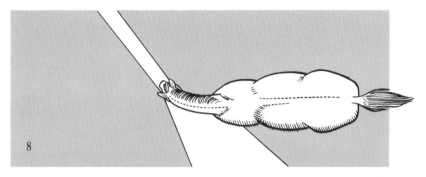

This illustration shows that a horse must turn his head sideways in order to be able to see his own hindquarters. To see over his back he must raise his head to where his eye would be above the level of his withers.

plains in part why horses will show anxiety and excitement from what appears to us to be sound coming from a harmless source since the horse has not brought into focus the origin of the sound.

Webster does not furnish such a word as "gotch" or "gotch-eyed" but the term is generally applied to the eye of any animal that does not set in exact focus with the other eye and is drawn to an improper position. An eye can be "gotched" at several angles. One of the three most common positions of a "gotch-eye" is for it to be pointed extremely outward as compared to the other eye which would prevent the horse from being able to focus a true picture at the proper rate of approach from that side. This being the case the horse will be approaching an object that will not come into focus until he is very near to it which would cause him to become suddenly aware of the object and dodge or shy. Many horses have been punished for being skittish when their vision was at fault and it was not their intention to be unruly. Illustration 9 shows this outward "gotch." Note the symbol of an object in front of this horse on that side which cannot be seen by the "gotched" eye.

Another "gotched" position is where the eyeball is turned downward and the circle of vision does not reach up into space sufficiently for the horse to be aware of trees, fences and other objects yet he would be ultra conscious of rocks, ditches or any object at a

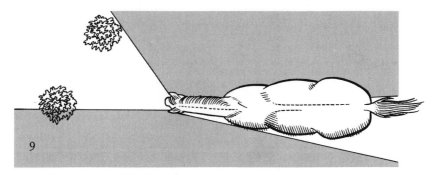

9

This illustration shows how the area of vision is reduced for a horse with a "gotch-eye." The white region just in front of him on the side of the bad eye is not visible to the horse. As he approaches an object it is very close to him before it comes within the scope of the "gotch-eye" and he is suddenly aware of it. In many instances this would cause a horse to shy.

low level. If he were a stock working horse, he would be guilty in many instances of passing a cow or horse without "turning back" because his visionary circle would be beneath the animal that he passed. This position of "gotch" will be accompanied by a showing of white between the dark color of the eye and the *upper* eyelid.

The third position of "gotch" is where the eyeball is turned upward and outward which prevents the horse from being able to see the ground where he is walking and enables him to get an unnecessary view of his rider and objects from his shoulder point upward. This position of "gotch" will be accompanied by a showing of white between the dark color of the eye and the *lower* eyelid.

Crossed eyes in horses are very common and in the days of mule breeding were more prevalent among mules than among horses. Crossed eyes always cause a horse to be uncertain of his footing and do a lot of snorting and object seriously to crossing bridges, railroad tracks and the like because of the fact that he constantly views two objects instead of one until he turns his head and takes a one-eyed picture of the object. A field, pasture or the bare earth are the only things that actually look natural to a cross-eyed horse.

Probably very few professional horsemen could determine the many positions of eyes and surely the beginner or amateur horseman would have almost no knowledge of the position of a horse's eyes. The most outward indication of any horse having visionary difficulties is the persistent way he will constantly work the ear on the side of his head where the eye is imperfect trying to hear the slightest sound and endeavoring to sense the origin of the sound. This ear will be alert and sensitive and upon examination with the human hand you can readily determine that the cartilage is extremely stiff and lacks the soft, velvety feel of a normal ear. As the horse grows older this will become a pricked ear because of the constant working of it backward and forward. Of course we all know that old horses are likely to be prick-eared; this could be due to age or it could be emphasized by both age and the impaired vision brought on by age. However, the presence of a pricked ear in young horses is invariably the indication of faulty vision.

Another type of eye that we have not heretofore discussed is commonly termed a "pig-eye." A "pig-eye" is small, set back in the head and generally is accompanied by thick eyelids. A "pig-eyed" horse has a much smaller area of circular vision and this type of eye generally denotes a nervous or stupid temperament.

If you have a horse that is in general use and is otherwise gentle and biddable that is subject to more than a common amount of "boogering" and "shying" from objects and terrain, it would be well for you to examine his eyes for proper position and defects before you attempt to whip and spur him out of his bad habits.

The Neck

THE NECK OF THE HORSE is given the least consideration by many horsemen when discussing the conformation of an individual horse. If the neck is not unsightly, there are many people who seldom reckon with its importance in judging a horse. I have often heard the remark of some horseman who says that he likes a "good" short neck. In some other group of horsemen the school of thinking is that they liked a "good" long neck. In my opinion there are no *good* short or *good* long necks. The horse's neck

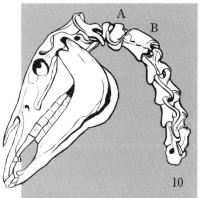

A *is the atlas vertebra of the neck that enables the horse to nod his head up and down without moving the rest of his neck and body.*

B *is the axis vertebra that enables the horse to turn his head to either side without moving his body.*

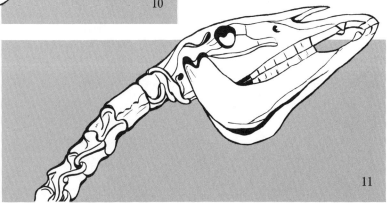

This illustration shows the position of a horse's head and neck when he has been jerked which locks both the atlas and axis vertebrae, and the horse is unable to move his head in any direction until the shock from being jerked subsides and pressure has ceased to be exerted against the horse's mouth. This same position causes a reverse contraction of the neck muscles that normally aid in moving the shoulders forward which clearly shows that a jerked horse in modern day terms is completely "out of gear" in his forequarters and cannot regain his balance and coordination until his head has been lowered and the atlas and axis vertebrae are in a moving position.

should be in ideal proportion to the size of his body, with due consideration to the purposes for which the horse is intended to be used, and taking into account the weight of the horse's head.

Those who can discuss the neck of a horse intelligently are truly horsemen of the old school. A horse's neck serves many purposes. First, the neck is important to the horse as a means of lowering his head to the level of the ground to graze and forage nourishment to sustain his body, and of reaching the water level of streams and lakes for his water supply. His neck is the manner by which his head is attached to his body, and the length of the neck and the degree of ideal conformation that the neck may possess determines greatly his power to use his head as a pendulum to shift the center of gravity of his own body and maintain balance in the event of adverse footing or emergencies caused by the confronting of foreign objects such as animals, trees, etc.

Since the eyes of a horse are mounted on each side of a wide forehead, and since his eyes take a side picture and are not placed in the front of his head, such as those of mankind, it is necessary that he be able to swing his head swiftly to either side or to raise his head in order to turn his head and look over his back. Since the horse must take pictures, so to speak, with each separate eye, and has a blind spot directly in front of him, it is highly important to his vision that his neck be flexible and capable of great degrees of angle and variation.

The first two vertebrae of the spine, which are attached to the skull and start the forming of the neck, are called the *Atlas vertebrae*. These two vertebrae are so constructed that they function by a slipping motion of the first *Atlas vertebra* over the second *Atlas vertebra*. This arrangement is the means whereby a horse is able to nod his head up and down forward, without moving the rest of his neck and body, which enables him to flex his poll, bow his neck and bring his chin under, which causes him to be much more maneuverable and gives him a greater handling ability on the bit, for whatever purposes he may be used by the rider.

The third and fourth vertebrae, which are the second pair of vertebrae in the horse's spine, enable him to swing his head to either side, as these two vertebrae work with each other in a manner similar to a hinge, and are called the *Axis vertebrae*. These are the vertebrae which enable a horse to shift his balance and aid his manner of traveling, as well as provide him with the ability for bringing objects in view as has heretofore been mentioned.

With the foregoing in mind, it is easy to determine that a short necked horse would have less actual use of his head and neck than

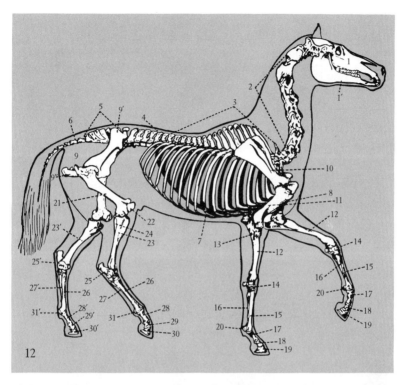

Skeleton of the horse, showing the vertebral arch and the bone columns, one pair of the legs supporting, the alternate pair partially flexed, in a stride. 1, bones of the head; 1', lower jaw; 2, cervical vertebrae; 3, dorsal vertebrae; 4, lumbar vertebrae; 5, sacral vertebrae (sacrum); 6, coccygeal vertebrae; 7, ribs; 8, sternum (breastbone); 9, pelvis; 9', ilium; 9", ischium; 10, scapula (shoulder blade); 11, humerus; 12, radius; 13, ulna; 14, carpus (knee); 15, large metacarpal bone (cannon); 16, small metacarpal bones (splint bones); 17, first phalanx (long pastern); 18, second phalanx (short pastern); 19, pedal bone (hoof bone); 20, proximal sesamoid bones; 21, femur; 22, patella (kneepan or -cap and stifle joint); 23, tibia; 24, fibula; 25, tarsus (hock); 26, large metatarsal bone (cannon); 27, small metatarsals (splint bones); 28, first phalanx (long pastern); 29, second phalanx (short pastern); 30, pedal bone (coffin bone); 31, proximal sesamoid bones. This illustration does not show the navicular bone, either front or rear legs. Other illustrations in this chapter show the location of the navicular or distal sesamoid bone.

a horse whose neck was of proper length in proportion to his body. And, by the same reckoning, an extremely long necked horse would have a loosely fitted head, and would lack coordination to carry the weight of his head and have proper pendulum strength to be used for balance.

Another most useful purpose for the horse's neck, which is seldom reckoned with by horsemen, is the fact that the muscles of the neck are the means by which a horse draws his shoulder and forelegs forward to produce stride. These neck muscles can contract and expand two-thirds of their natural length, which would readily explain why a short necked horse (and this neck is generally accompanied by a short shoulder) would have a short stride, and would be more subject to stumbling and less capable of using his forelegs in a versatile manner.

Now the argument against an extremely long neck is that these muscles might well be underdeveloped, and would be subject to early fatigue under hard use. Quite often a weak neck-muscled horse will tire readily, and as he does so, you may well notice how droopily he will carry his head and neck and what weak and uneven motion will be produced by his forelegs.

Necks should be looked at and examined on the basis of their usefulness. A neck well arched, with a nice, flat, level place just behind the ears, where the skull is attached, belongs to a horse of good balance and vision. The desirability of the length of the neck can often be determined at a glance by the carriage of the head and the manner in which the neck is fitted into the withers. And to further define the area of the neck, it might well be stated here that it is generally considered to be the vertebra just in front of the withers of the horse and extending just behind the poll of the head, where the first Atlas vertebra is attached to the skull.

Another thing to be considered, which can be determined by the eye and by examination with the hand, is that the muscling of the neck should adhere well to the spine and have an upwardlike formation following the crest of the neck. This leaves an open area at the base of the neck for the free expansion of the windpipe for taking in an abundance of air, and should leave a well-defined valley between the windpipe and the muscled area, where a large jugular vein can be carried without undue pressure from the muscled area.

It is the conception among most horsemen that locomotion is derived from the power of the hindquarters. This, to a degree, is true; but the ability of the horse to properly spread that locomotion over the ground in front of him is greatly controlled by the movement of the shoulders and the forelegs. This movement is greatly enhanced and, to a degree, controlled by the muscling of the neck. In the final furlong of many races, the horse with the greatest ability of his neck muscles to draw his forequarters forward to the greatest stride will be the winner.

The undesirable necks to watch for, which can be determined with the naked eye, are too thick, beefy necks; extremely thin, long necks, where the head is not properly attached to the *Atlas vertebrae;* and *ewe* necks that appear to have been put on the horse bottom-side-up. (This type of neck causes the horse to be high headed, with poor vision, poor bitting and reining ability, and dangerous as to the manner in which he uses his forefeet to cover the ground, besides being the ugliest of all horses.)

In the selection of mares for breeding purposes, necks should show refinement, with clean-cut throatlatches and be feminine in appearance. Coarse necked mares, especially those that carry heavy crests, as a rule are poor breeders and difficult to get in foal. Stallions should show strong, masculine necks, with exceptionally good muscling. A well-arched neck is highly desirable and some crest is desirable. However, over-crested stallions have a coarsened appearance and give additional weight to the front end of the horse without serving any useful purpose. Thin, marelike necks on stallions are objectionable and such horses should be gelded.

It would also be well to note in this article that in the selection of ponies for children, ladies and other light riders, crested necks are usually objectionable because ponies of such conformation are usually *pullers* and hard mouthed.

Necks, when fit onto properly sloped shoulders of good length, appear to be in balance with the rest of the horse. In the case of short, straight-shouldered horses, the neck sometimes appears coarse because there is no length of shoulder extending toward the ground beyond the bottom line of the neck. Sometimes these horses' necks are not objectionable, and it is the lack of shoulder that causes them to appear so.

The Spine

THROUGHOUT MANKIND'S EFFORTS to improve the horse, if there had ever been a definite means of producing a well-bred or near-perfect spine, it might easily be said that you would have the near-perfect body of a horse.

Since the spine is the trunk, which the rest of the horse is suspended from or attached to, its contours and substance are of utmost importance to the general conformation of the horse.

The now commonly called Cerebric vertebrae (which constitutes the neck) consists of seven in number. The first two are the Atlas vertebrae which enable the horse to nod his head up and down. The second pair are the Axis vertebrae which enable the horse to turn his head back and forth sideways, and are a part of the total number of the seven Cerebric vertebrae.

The vertebrae of the back, which are the Dorsal vertebrae, are eighteen in number. The first five are the vertebrae of the withers. The remaining thirteen constitute the rest of the length of back to the beginning of the Lumbar vertebrae just under the loin. The Lumbar vertebrae really belong to the back, which makes a total of twenty-four. The Sacral vertebrae (those of the rump lying between the haunch bone and the tailhead) are five in number and the Caudel vertebrae (those of the tail) are fifteen in number, making a grand total of fifty-one vertebrae in the horse's body.

The main nerves for the entire body follow the spinal column from the central nervous system, which is the brain, and have their outlets into the body between each of the vertebrae, which are cushioned with elastic cartilage commonly referred to as discs, that prevent the pinching of the nerves in their course of travel out of the spine. The spine also houses the principal quantity of the marrow of the horse, which is part of the blood-producing mechanism of the body.

The ribs are suspended from the spinal column. The first eight of them, which are true ribs in that they are attached at the bottom to the breast bone, form the thorax which affords the area for the attachment of the shoulders and forelegs. The last ten ribs form a protecting shelter over the rest of the internal organs.

The pelvic bones are attached to the spinal column, which forms the connection for the hindquarters and hind legs. The muscular development of the loins and hindquarters is greatly influenced by the development and perfection, or the lack of same, of the spine.

The pattern of length in the vertebrae in making up the spine is the all-deciding factor in the pattern of top line of the horse. When the Cerebric vertebrae of the neck are of a long pattern, the shoulders will be well laid back, in order to be joined to the withers' Dorsal vertebrae, which would constitute a desirable length of neck, sloped shoulders and short back. This conformation is desirable in that it would produce a horse of long stride, maneuverable head and neck and short Dorsal vertebrae, which would contribute to the horse's ability to carry weight. If the Cerebric vertebrae of the neck are inclined to be of short structure, the neck will be short and the shoulders will be formed short and straight, causing the back to be long, all of which is undesirable in a useful horse.

After a study of the skeleton of a horse, it can readily be seen that an ideally constructed spine would be the first prerequisite to an ideal body of a horse.

The spine is very flexible in young horses. Horses in hard use that are more than ten years old will quite often have many of the vertebrae of the back (Dorsal) fused together which greatly reduces the flexibility of the spine. A horse, at any age, is never endowed with the flexibility of the spine which many other animals possess.

Horsemen have always looked at young foals and discussed their good and bad qualities and what kind of horses they would or would not make. To my thinking, the only positive opinions that can be had of a young foal are those regarding the ratio of the top line which is, of course, determined by the bone pattern of the spine. Foals with a desirable length of shoulders and short backs will have the same comparative top line conformation when they are developed horses. Short necked, long backed foals will grow into horses of that pattern. The spine is the one part of a foal that will remain in its same proportions.

There has been a practice among old horsemen, since the beginning of time, of feeling the spine at the tailhead, where the spine comes out of the body, to determine if the horse had a large spine or one of lesser size. This custom may have meant something to horsemen but, to my knowledge, there has never been any set size that this part of the spine should be in relation to the weight or size of the horse, and I have never been able to justify the practice as being of any definite use. It can be assumed, from the lack of more positive knowledge, that the size of bone structure of the spine is in keeping with the body bone development of the horse. This may or may not be true and is yet to be proven.

The Thorax

THE THORAX OF THE HORSE is often referred to as the "barrel," "middle" or sometimes "trunk." It is difficult to determine what is the most important bone, muscle or region of a horse, and I would hesitate to define or describe any such region as being the *most important,* when we take into consideration the fact that a sesamoid bone, mounted behind the ankle and forming a part of the ankle joint, weighs only a very few ounces, but when it is cracked or otherwise injured, a thousand-pound horse is lame and unuseful. Therefore, it cannot be said that any particular region of the body is the most important part.

But, to be sure, the thorax is among the most vital regions of the animal body. It is formed by the spine at the top and the ribs on each side, with the cartilage and breastbone at the bottom. This thorax is not positively attached to the shoulders in any manner other than by muscles and it is suspended at the bottom from the side of the forelegs by muscle attachments as shown in Illustration 13. By this means of suspension, a *shock absorbing* effect is produced which greatly reduces the jar to the organs housed within the thorax, these principally being the heart and lungs.

Horses and men have been described as having *heart* to do something, or not having *heart* to do something. I believe all horsemen will agree that the last furlong of a race, or the last polo chucker, or the last and highest jump, are done on *heart*. And any old cowboy knows that horses have run up on wild broncos to give the rider a throw with the rope, or have caught a mean bull or a wild steer in the brush at the top of a mountain, long after all common standards of endurance were supposed to have been exhausted. Whatever phrases or terminology have been applied to horses in regard to heart, of course were intended to describe their *staying* ability, above and beyond the common performance of average horses.

We talk about girth, heart, and room for heart and lungs, when we actually mean that we need an abundance of room for lungs; because I doubt seriously that any horse has actually had too small a space for his heart.

The heart is held in a stable position within the thorax and it performs a marvelous and unbelievable amount of physical exertion, almost beyond the power of the human mind to understand. The weight of most any light-boned, performance-bred horse is one-eighth blood, which means that a one thousand-pound horse has one hundred twenty-five pounds of blood, or equivalent to about fifteen gallons. The heart pumps this fifteen gallons at the rate of about thirty-two to thirty-four beats per minute, and about twenty-eight to thirty-two ounces per beat, which is roughly about a quart. These figures, extended into a hard day's work, mean that the heart beats 48,000 times and pumps 12,230 to 12,240 gallons of blood per day. This center of the circulatory system is responsible for the conveyance of energy-producing properties of the blood to revitalize the muscular strength of the animal.

The real need for room in the thorax is for an abundance of lungs, in order that a good supply of oxygen can be furnished to the blood circulating through the lungs, and in order that the horse may have a reserve supply of wind for exhaling. Since a horse cannot refill his lungs under stress, he must do the work assigned to him with the oxygen that has already been inhaled and is available for the purposes of the body. There is little more than twenty percent of the available air in a horse's lungs that can be breathed out when the horse is relaxed, which is referred to as "tidal" air. When the horse is under stress, if he has a large, wide rib spring, it would give him an exceptionally big diaphragm and, provided that the muscling of his belly walls and flanks is adequate, this tidal air could be increased to the ratio of from twenty-eight percent to as much as thirty-two percent. This increase of exhale is produced by a bellows-like action of the diaphragm while the horse is in motion. Since the diaphragm could be no wider than the rib spring, this is a clear explanation of the need for rib spring to produce tidal air to be used under stress. The remainder of the air in the horse's lungs is constantly being used up by the circulating blood that is extracting the oxygen content to be supplied to the muscle system.

We know that the given amount of space required to house the actual working units (heart, lungs, arteries, windpipe, etc.), together with the ribs, cartilage, muscle and skin, is about fifty-two inches (measured at the girth) for a horse 14.2 hands tall—provided, of course, he is of reasonable proportions. The next additional ten inches of measurement does not afford a great ratio percentage of air intake. The second ten inches of additional girth measurement would greatly increase the percentage of space for air intake, which means that the minimum measurement of the girth on a horse of this height should be not less than seventy-two inches. Each additional inch thereafter, which will be gained because of the horse's favorable conformation, will greatly increase the horse's intake of air and *staying* ability.

With the foregoing needs for space in the thorax of a horse in mind, it can readily be understood that slab-sided horses, with

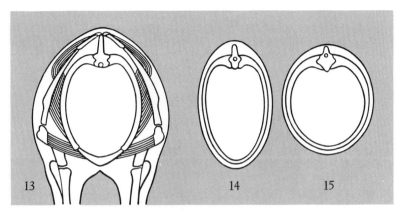

Ideal shape thorax—large heart and lung capacity inside, large area outside for muscular attachment of shoulders, legs, etc.

"Slab-side"   *"Round" cylinder*

poor rib spring (as shown in Illustration 14) would not be horses of great *staying* ability. Such poor rib spring also greatly reduces the horse's ability to carry weight. This type of rib spring is not as comfortable to the rider, and makes it harder for a rider to maintain the balance of his body above the horse's back, because his legs are too close together due to the thinness of the horse between them.

Another undesirable rib spring is the round, cylinder type (as shown in Illustration 15). These ribs appear to be well sprung, but the ribs do not carry down a sufficient length along the sides. This type of thorax, or *barrel,* leaves quite a lot of daylight showing under the horse and decreases his ability for balance because of his legginess.

Illustration 13 shows the ideal type of rib spring, extending well out from the spine, affording a good base on top to carry weight, and the contour providing an abundance of lung and heart capacity. This type of rib spring also contributes to the ability of a horse to forage a greater amount of roughage and affords him a roomier digestive system, which is less susceptible to colic and other digestive disorders.

In close observance of this ideal type of thorax development, the naked eye could appraise a horse by looking from the floor of the body at the cinch to the ground, then looking from the floor of the body to the top of the withers. The distance should be as near the same as possible. Then, standing in front of the horse, hold his head and neck in line with his spine and look down the side of the horse, at a level about equivalent to the position of the cinch ring of your saddle. At this view you should see a well extended side of the horse, beyond the position of his shoulders. If the horse that appeared to have depth of body is slab-sided, it is objectionable. The point that I want to make is that you cannot always tell about the abundance of rib spring from looking at the horse from a perpendicular position. The round, cylinder barreled horses that appear to have an abundance of rib spring, but whose ribs do not carry down far enough, will be easily detected because of the extreme amount of daylight left under them and the appearance of legginess.

Last, but not least, the thorax is the *assembly point,* so to speak, whereby the shoulders and forelegs are attached to the horse's body, and the neck, together with its windpipe, jugular vein, spinal column and main nerves from the central nervous system (the brain) are received into the body of the horse.

It can be readily understood that the more perfectly the rib spring and over-all thorax is formed, the greater the area will be that is provided for the proper fixation of the shoulder, leg and neck muscles to be attached to the body.

Shoulders

EVER SINCE MAN BEGAN TO RIDE HORSES there has always been some farsighted horseman who has endeavored to understand the mechanism of the horse. Man has always been prompted to try to improve his domestic animals for his own comfort or financial benefit.

The shoulders of horses have been discussed in literature by the horsemen of the different ages and much has been said about the length and position of shoulders. In the early writings on horses by the Mongolians and the Arabs, significant note was made of the "line" of the shoulder. In early English writings in the late 1700s, the remark was that a shoulder should be "oblique." In recent writings, authorities on horses have always stated that a shoulder should be "well laid back," and in modern American writings up to the turn of the century, much has been said about the "slope" of the shoulder. Even in recent magazines, published in the last few years, there have been diagrams in standing positions with a line drawn from the slope of the shoulder down to the ground to show the extended reach of the forefoot. There have been numerous horse authorities through the ages, all agreeing that shoulders should be "laid back," "sloped," "oblique," etc., but to my own personal knowledge, I have never found an article that has shown why this is a mechanical fact in the anatomy of a horse.

In the accompanying sketch, Illustration 16 shows the bone structure of the shoulder and the foreleg in a straight, standing position. You will note in this example the opening at the front of the lower point of the scapula, which to us is the shoulder blade. You will note the extended bone structure at the upper outside point of the humerus. These two points form what we refer to as the point of the shoulder.

Illustration 17 shows this same shoulder and foreleg in a reaching position, which illustrates how the extended upper point of the humerus fits into the lower outside point of the scapula. This causes a locked position which determines the reach of the horse and will be an explanation as to why all horsemen through the ages have agreed that shoulders should be sloped back.

A casual study of this drawing will show any observer that by drawing the shoulder blade forward to a straightened position, the "gap" between the lower point of the scapula and the upper outer point of the humerus will be reduced. This means that you are shortening the radius that the foot may be moved by reason of the fact that there is less leverage left in the "gap" at the face of the shoulder blade. When a shoulder is brought forward, it is by

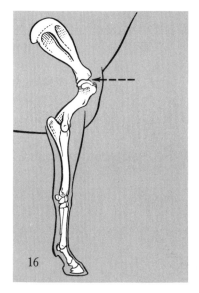
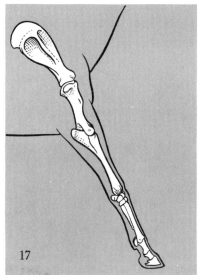

"Gap" in shoulder.   *Shoulder locked.*

necessity, due to the depth of the body, made shorter. The same reasoning applies whereby the greater the slope the longer the shoulder because the depth of the body would allow more length.

This should be an explanation to most horsemen that a shoulder should not be shorter than the length of the horse's head, measuring from the top of his poll, a straight line down his face to the base of the nostril. For argument's sake, this line will be an average of twenty-four inches long. When the shoulder is measured from the top of the shoulder blade just beneath the withers to the point of the shoulder, a good, normal slope would be equivalent to the length of the head. A greater length would mean an increased stride and/or a greater depth of body, either of which would be very desirable.

There are other advantages to be gained by great length and slope of shoulder. The shoulder of a horse is attached to the body (thorax) by muscle, cartilage, ligaments, and over all covered by the skin. There is no actual "bone joint" attachment holding the shoulder to the body. A long, sloping shoulder distributes this attachment over a greater area. The strain produced by jar and friction is distributed by the muscular attachments in a manner that will be resistant to stiffening of the shoulders. The contrast to this in a short shoulder means that the muscles themselves must become more taut and overdeveloped to withstand the corresponding amount of jar and the cartilage and ligaments become more fibered, which results in the "stiffening" of the shoulders from the various abuses that a horse must endure in racing and performance events.

This favorable anatomy on the forequarters enables the horse to be more maneuverable with his forefeet and more capable of coping with the uneven terrain that he is forced to travel over. This position also adds to the comfort of the rider inasmuch as the friction of contact with the earth is deflected at more points and since the upper part of the shoulder blade is attached to the body at the withers, the withers will be well set back from a direct line over the foreleg which removes the rider from a great deal of jar. There is also a great benefit to the horse himself in that the sloped shoulder places the rider in the "spring" of the horse's back and does not allow the strain of burden to come down on the knees and ankles at such a direct and pounding line.

Forelegs

IT HAS BEEN COMMONLY THOUGHT through the ages of horsemanship that the primary function of the foreleg was to "hold the horse up." This, of course, to a large extent is true but forelegs cannot be dismissed with such a simple statement in view of the fact that the balance of a horse is greatly determined by the position of his head and neck, and the position of the forelegs in relation to the balance of the body.

Before the invention of motion pictures, it was thought that the foreleg had no pulling power and that the horse's body was propelled forward by the muscle structure of the hindquarters. After studying motion pictures of horses in action it can well be deter-

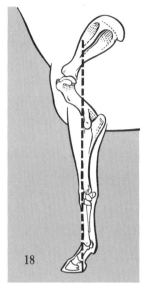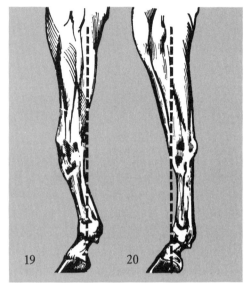

mined that the foreleg does pull enough weight forward in motion to keep the top line of the horse directed in a forward course. It is also the muscling and function of the foreleg that contributes to the actual stride of a horse in motion.

Since the principle purpose of the foreleg is to hold up weight, it must be so constructed that this duty can be performed with the greatest possible ease and efficiency without damage to the mechanism of the foreleg by continuous use or undue abuse. So in considering the construction of the foreleg, from a side view the bone structure should be almost perpendicular to the underline of the body as shown in Illustration 18. This, a good shaped foreleg, will enable the animal to travel forward with greater ease to the horse and to the rider, and have a minimum amount of damage to the bone structure of the leg.

The most objectionable positions of forelegs that are commonly seen in horses are:

(1) "Buck-kneed" as shown in Illustration 19. A buck-kneed horse is carrying the tendons and muscles, as well as the bone structure of the foreleg, in the position of a horse that is traveling downhill. This is a constant position of improper balance and a

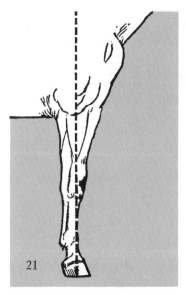
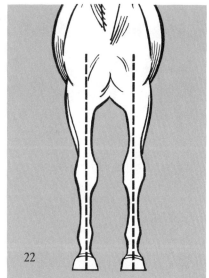

21

22

foreleg that is buck-kneed is more susceptible to stumbling and falling by breaking over at the knees. This position of the foreleg also induces the development of side bones near the heel of the foot.

(2) The next most serious and common position of the foreleg is generally described as "calf-kneed," which means that the knee is bent backward, away from a straight line between the ankle and the upper part of the forearm, as shown in Illustration 20. This position of the foreleg causes the horse to carry the muscle and tendon structure of the leg in a constant position that would be compared to a horse traveling uphill. It contributes to a pounding gait as the horse places his foot back to the ground, and is a contributing factor to the unsoundness of the pastern joint and ankle. A horse that is calf-kneed also has less pulling power in his forelegs in that there is a decided weakness at the pisiform bone which is the little bone that sticks out at the back of the knee. A calf-kneed horse also is more likely to suffer damage to ligaments and tendons of the foreleg.

(3) A very common improper position of the foreleg is a leg that stands too straight from the knee through the ankle and

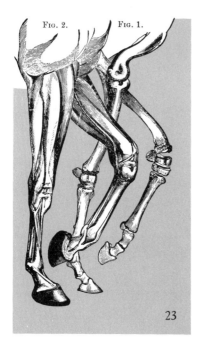

FIG. 2.   FIG. 1.

The arrangement and shape of the several bones will be readily understood. A large, flat knee is essential in the horse, since it not only carries plenty of integument, but allows free play to this portion of the leg. Fig. 1 shows the knee flexed and Fig. 2 the knee at rest.

23

24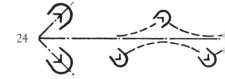

through the pastern joint to the ground as shown in Illustration 21. This leg has very little spring action and causes a short, choppy gait and a very jarring effect to the rider. Unsoundness will occur from the lack of leverage in the pastern which will cause wind galls at the angle and breaking over at the knee.

The front position of the foreleg should be exactly straight, where a straight line could be drawn from the point of the shoulder through the center of the knee joint, continuing down through the center of the ankle, and through the point of the toe as shown in Illustration 22. Any variance from this straight line pattern of the foreleg causes splints to form on the inside of the leg and may cause possible damage to the angles. Also any horse with a degree of variance from this pattern, either in or out, will have some difficulty in the handling of the forefeet and will either be splay footed and paddle, or wing, neither of which is conducive to a straight forward movement or the most advantageous use of the forefeet in maintaining balance of the body in motion.

All horses at the walk and trot should be able to rock their front feet upward from the heel, break them over squarely at the toe, carry them forward in a straight line and set them down again. It is impossible for a splay-footed horse to carry his front feet straight forward. Study the adjacent diagram and learn why the splay-footed position in horses is objectionable. The following statements supply the answer.

1. The splay-footed position on the front feet predisposes to faulty action and results in a defect in gait known as dishing or winging in.

2. Winging in is a defect in gait that predisposes to interference. Toe wide horses quite commonly hit their ankles, their shins or their knees.

3. Interference predisposes to blemish or unsoundness.

4. Blemishes and unsoundnesses depreciate the value of a horse, thereby affecting the economics of the horse business. Hence the reason why there should be sharp discrimination against splay-footed horses.

The illustration shows course taken by a front foot in case of toe-wide or splay-footed horses.

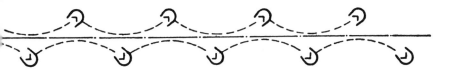

There are many examples of pigeon-toed, knock-kneed and bow-kneed horses as well as toes that stand too close in at the ground or two wide out at the ground. Any variance from the pattern of a straight foreleg has its contributing handicap and in most instances there is no advantage to be gained from improper position of the forelegs.

One of the most objectionable and most common faults in the foreleg of the present-day horse is the splay-footed position of the forefeet as shown in Illustration 24. The diagram plainly shows how much interference could be caused by this splay-footed action where the heels and ankles of the opposite forefoot are continually in danger of being bruised or cut or even stepped on to the extent of causing stumbling or falling. Whatever arguments might be advanced as to the shoeing or trimming of feet, there is no denying that straight forelegs with good, sound bone structure and big, flat knees with deep, well shaped ankles, are the most desirable limbs that can perform the duty of holding up the front end of a horse and provide him with necessary equipment for swift, clean action and durable soundness.

Pasterns

LITTLE CONCERN IS SHOWN by most people over the length, angle and slope of the pastern joint of a horse. In the discussion of legs among amateurish horse people, and even some of those who have been in the horse business several years, when you mention the pastern it is a very common occurence to have to describe the region of the foreleg or hindleg where the pastern joints are fixed between the foot and the ankle.

The construction of the pastern joint exerts a greater influence on the soundness of the leg joints above it than do any of the other joints affect the function of the pastern.

The pastern joint serves several purposes in the handling of the legs of a horse and a perfect pastern contributes greatly to the spring and action that a horse may be endowed with. It also has a very determining effect on the soundness of the ankles, knees and hocks.

In Illustration 25 you have the ideal length pastern, mounted at a very desirable angle. This pastern is straight enough to prevent damage to the ankle when the horse is coming back to the earth with the weight of his body striking the ground. This angle of pastern will prevent the ankle from being injured by preventing it from striking the ground and at the same time will give sufficient leverage to act as a *shock absorber* to the ankle joint, the knee and the rest of the horse's body, even to the extent of reducing shock to the rider on top of the horse's back.

This good pastern also enables the horse to have sufficient leverage below the ankle joint to maneuver over rough terrain with a minimum amount of effort, which will contribute to his ability to endure hard rides over terrain of undesirable footing.

This ideal pastern also equips the horse with a desirable amount

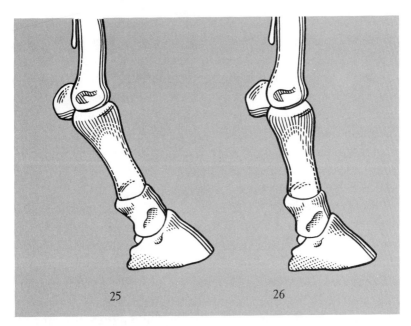

25   26

Ideal length pastern, mounted at a   *Short, straight pastern.*
desirable angle.

of cat-like spring when the muscle structure, ligaments and tendons are contracted to cause a hurling of the body forward in the beginning of a sprint movement.

In the discussion of pasterns with cowboys and people who have performance horses the opinion is quite often stated that a *short* pastern is by far the best for the many versatile uses of a working horse. I doubt that any persons advancing such a statement actually mean that they want a *short* pastern; they are, in fact, trying to emphasize that they do not want a *long* pastern.

Illustration 26 shows a *short* pastern. This pastern is in a position almost erect and nearly in line with the cannon and forearm. This type is always accompanied by so-called *wind-galls*. *Wind-galls* are never seen on a horse that hasn't been worked and the reason for a so-called *wind-gall* is the sharp pounding against the small gland which secretes a lubricating substance known as *synovia*. This lubricating fluid will be secreted excessively where the glands are irritated by constant jarring. This fluid lubricates the region where the tendons pass around the sesamoid bone at the back of the ankle to reduce friction of the tendons in their movement back and forth across the sesamoid and along the tendon track immediately behind the pastern joint and cannon bone. The excessive amount of fluid that is produced is deposited in small pockets at the back of the ankle and is referred to as *wind-gall* because it is soft and moveable. Had this pastern not been short the excessive irritation would not have occurred and these *wind-galls* would not have been developed by the deposits of synovia.

This direct stroke of friction also causes the knee joint to be inclined to buck forward and in time renders the horse *buck-kneed* which reduces the maneuverability of the knee, shortens his ability for stride and contributes to the incidents of falling.

The severe pounding on the center joint of the pastern in time will cause excessive calcification to occur, stiffening and enlarging the joint and creating pain in the cartilage and muscle structure of the joint. This excessive pounding which causes such positive and direct friction at the joint because of the lack of leverage in the pastern contributes greatly to the development of side bones and enlargements of the distal sesamoid bone which is mounted just above the hoof and under the lower joint of the pastern.

A horse suffering these accumulated injuries brought on by hard use is referred to as *walking on pin cushions*. He is subject to being constantly sore in the forelegs and is of little service while he is still a reasonably young horse.

I found a family of these horses on the West Coast, all having excessive calcification at the joint of the pastern and all having bucked knees. All horses of this family that I saw were subject to stumbling and falling and were of little use in spite of the ideal measurements and conformation of their bodies. This type of pastern is also rough riding to the man on the horse's back.

Among race horse people there is the misconception of the advantages to be had from a *long* pastern as shown in Illustration 27. Contrary to the belief of most people the length of this pastern does not contribute to the springing stride of a horse in galloping

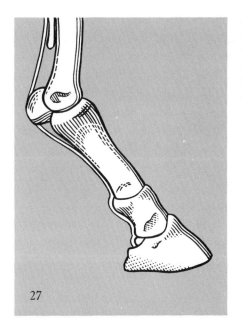

Long, sloping pastern. (Note the tendon that runs along the back of the leg which, due to the excessive length and slope of the pastern, exerts greater pressure on the sesamoid bone.)

27

motion. This pastern, being much too long, is easily weakened due to the undesirable angle and under stress and strain will allow the ankles to be bruised against the ground and severe damage will sometimes be caused to the protruding regions of the sesamoid bones which are mounted at the back of the ankles.

The sesamoid is mounted crossways at the back of the ankle joint and is so shaped that the center of it forms a pulley-like groove which is used by the tendons in the rapid movement from the foot around the ankle and up to the hock joint, etc. A *long* pastern causes severe pressure to be exercised against the center of the sesamoid bone when the horse is running at terrific speed. The lead leg in a race horse catches approximately eighteen hundred pounds of weight jar when he is running at a *winning* rate of speed. The pressure brought to bear by the tendons on the sesamoid because of the extended length of pastern is what *cracks* sesamoids.

Cracked sesamoids have become a common cause in the disabling of prominent race horses and it would well behoove the Thoroughbred breeders to take better account of the length of pastern and the size of the ankles in an effort to breed horses with legs to stand the stress and strain of speed and carrying weight.

Long pasterns also contribute to the incidents of bowed tendons.

A slight difference in the length of the front and back pastern is desirable. The back pastern should be ten percent longer than the front pastern in order that it will be positioned at the same angle. It is a common deficiency in the locomotive structure of a horse's legs for the back pastern to be the same length as the front pastern in which case the horse will seldom have as desirable a stride in the reach of the back leg as he has in the reach of the foreleg. Short pasterns of the back leg also are prone to add to the possibility of breaking over or stumbling of the back feet.

Extremes in the anatomy of a horse take their toll on soundness and durability. A careful study of balance in the bone structure of legs could contribute a great deal to the breeding of more desirable horses for the future.

The cowboy needs to become better acquainted with the undesirable effects of *short* pasterns and the race horse breeder needs to take account of the unsoundness caused by the excessive length of pastern, either of which are not in balance with the rest of the bone structure of the horse's legs.

Hindquarters

THE HINDQUARTERS OF A HORSE, other than for the purpose of standing, serve an entirely different purpose to the horse than his forelegs. Where the shoulders and forelegs are attached to the spine and thorax only by a spring-like system of muscles, the hindquarters are firmly attached to the spine by the pelvis bones. Then the hip bones, stifles, etc. are attached to the pelvis bones. This empowers the hindquarters to have a direct and positive force in moving the body forward. Since the hindquarters do not take a large amount of severe shock, this firm attachment at the spine has no detrimental effect (whereas the forelegs do take a tremendous

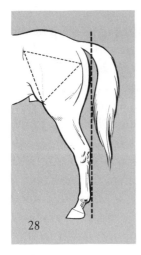 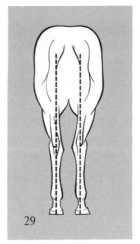 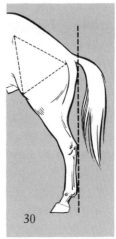

28   29   30

Proper position of hind-
quarter and leg from
side view.

Proper position of hind-
quarters and legs from
rear view.

Goose rump

amount of concussion that could not be endured if they were
firmly affixed).

The intricate muscular formation of the hindquarters, stifle and
gaskin is so technical (and, after all, the exact development of the
muscling of the hindquarters is well portrayed by the exterior appearance of the hindquarters) that we will deal with the conformation of the hindquarters as observed by the naked eye.

For the most useful purposes, and the most pleasing to the eye, is
a firm coupling of the pelvis bones, where they are attached to the
spine, with a slight arch over the loins and continuing on into the
hindquarters. When the coupling is in proper position to the hip
bones, it should be in a line between the hip bones on each side of
the horse. This position of the coupling might vary slightly forward, or slightly backward, without any serious malformation of
the horse. However, it has been my observation, and I am convinced beyond all reasonable doubt, that mares which have a coupling severely *offset* to the rear of this position seldom have good
pelvis bones. The pelvis bones of mares with such coupling do not
have the normal amount of flexibility, therefore, it is common for

such mares to have difficulty in delivering their foals.

An ideal length of hindquarters, measured along the top of the hindquarters from the coupling to a line even with the cheek of the rump, should not be less than two-thirds of the length of the back; and, of course, additional length is desirable.

An ideal hindquarter, for a performance type horse, should contain a perfect triangle, measured from the point of the hip to the seam of the muscling above the cheek bone of the rump, back down to the dimple of the stifle joint, then across the flank from the stifle, back to the hip bone (as in Illustration 28). The reason for this being the ideal hindquarter can be readily understood when it is realized that the horse in motion does not *push* his body forward by a simple movement. The tendons are drawn to start the foot pressing against the earth and that motion goes through the pastern and ankle to the hock joint. From the hock joint it is transmitted to the point of the dimple of the stifle in the fore part of the hind leg, just below the flank. From this point, the muscling is so attached to the stifle that a play of energy goes from the stifle joint, backward toward the cheek of the rump, then forward over the top line of the hindquarter, and this motion moves the horse forward. Any variance, or loss of measurement, in the aforementioned triangle will result in a loss of the ideal balance and force of the muscle action of the hindquarter.

A reasonable amount of width in the hindquarters is necessary in order to put the stifles wide enough apart to have room for good development, and in order that the hocks and the lower part of the legs may be set at a desirable distance from each other, so the hocks and feet will not interfere with each other in motion (see Illustration 29).

Since the stifle is the beginning power of the hindquarter in rolling the body forward, the stifle muscles should be well-developed and well-brought-down from behind, from the cheek of the rump toward the hock. Stifles should be well-developed inside the horse's leg as well as the outside.

The gaskin muscles, which are formed on the tibia bone just above the hock, do not exert the greatest amount of force in sending the body forward in the beginning of stride. The muscling of the gaskin has, in a large degree, the control of the course that the leg follows in its forward movement, provided that the bone structure is in good alignment.

A gaskin that is heavily muscled inside the leg, with flat muscles on the outside of the leg, will draw the leg in as the horse moves forward, which oftentimes results in the foot's cutting the opposite hind leg above the ankle. This same movement may sometimes cause the toes of the back feet to cut the tendons and the back portion of the forelegs. The opposite to this muscling, where the outside gaskin muscles are extremely heavy and the inside of the gaskin is flat and not sufficiently muscled, will cause a horse in motion to travel wide. And, standing behind a horse with this type of muscling, the forefeet and legs can oftentimes be seen in full view when the horse is in motion.

The gaskin that is well-muscled, both inside and out, with good alignment of bone structure, will cause the hind legs to follow the exact pattern of movement of the forelegs, and gives the horse much greater balance, reducing the possibilities of injury and reducing the incidence of unsoundness.

The final performance of the gaskin muscles in action is very important in that these muscles make the final movement that completely straightens out the back leg, which increases the springiness of the galloping or trotting movement of the horse.

Hocks are the levers of the hind leg which permit the free flowing of energy from the feet to the hindquarter muscling. Hocks take a tremendous amount of abuse from all performance activities of a horse. Hocks that set *wide* form a turning-out movement in motion, and hocks that are set close together, often referred to as *cow hocks,* cause the horse's feet to be pointed outward in traveling, sometimes referred to as *coon-footed.* (For further information, refer to the article in this text on hocks.)

There are several types of hindquarters that are undesirable, and are easily observed by the naked eye.

The *goose-rumped* horse, as shown in Illustration 30, is one where the line from the coupling to the cheek of the rump slopes

37

off severely, and the peak of the buttocks is set too low toward the hock and too near an even line from the flank to the cheek of the buttock. The top line of this hindquarter will not be able to properly utilize the power generated by the stifle in moving the animal's body forward.

Extremely short hindquarters are always objectionable. Wide, thick, beefy hindquarters, as viewed from the rear, to some people are beautiful, however, such hindquarters belong to horses of slow motion and pulling drive, such as in the case of draft horses. Extremely narrow hindquarters are not desirable in any horse since this would cause a loss of the proper alignment of the bone structure and a sacrifice of power and soundness.

Another hindquarter appearance that is considered objectionable by some people is the extremely high set of the tail. The top line of the rump on such horses is straight from the coupling to the tailset and might give the appearance of the horses' having a flat coupling, which actually is not the case—it has a high tailset. Although this top line of hindquarter is considered objectionable by many, such hindquarters were greatly prized by the early-day Asiatic and Arabian breeders. A high tailset of this description may not be entirely pleasing to the naked eye, but it is no real, serious defect of conformation and no loss of power in the hindquarter is suffered by a high tailset.

In observing a horse, quite often one makes the mistake of being impressed by beautiful hindquarters. It is well that a horse has beautiful hindquarters, that are well-shaped, sound and capable of producing force and energy. But, after all is said in regard to hindquarters, shoulders, front and back legs of a horse, it must be borne in mind that the horse must have balance between the conformation and soundness of the forequarters, and the conformation and soundness of the hindquarters, in order to be able to move in a desirable manner with the least possible damage to the animal's body, and one should guard against overestimating the value of hindquarters alone.

Hocks

AFTER ALL THE PROS AND CONS and likes and dislikes of horsemen in the discussion of hocks, *there is just one good hock on a horse and there is just one good position and height of hocks.* Hocks have been discussed since the beginning of horsemanship and much has been said and a good deal has been done to produce horses with good, sound, straight, usable hocks, especially in the days when man's way of life depended on a horse. A horse's maneuverability of all portions of the body in his efforts to leave the ground is greatly controlled by the soundness, strength and quality of the hocks.

LOW HOCKS

The remark is quite often heard among horsemen, especially "cutting" and other performance horsemen, including polo, jumpers, etc., that they like a low hock. The question arises in my mind as to who knows where *low* starts and where *high* starts and what angle or position is a *low* hock. The naked eye knows very little about a *low* or a *high* hock. For argument's sake, we will assume that the distance from the top of the rump to the ground is the same on three horses. The position of the hock is not going to change the horse's height at the rump. Therefore, the only way you can lower his hock would be to *lengthen* the tibia bone, which is the *long* bone from the stifle to the hock and *shorten* the cannon bone from the hock to the ankle. In so doing, you will have a horse with his hock in the position shown in Illustration 34. This *low* hock by reason of the length of the tibia bone from the stifle to the hock, places the hock out from under the horse's body and is not in a straight line from the cheek of his rump to the point of his hock, a position which good balance demands. The only way to get this hock under the horse would be to "sickle" the leg severely from the point of the hock to the point of the ankle, which would place the ankle and the pastern under severe strain, and put the hock in a crooked, grotesque position. This *low* hock reduces the muscular ability in the hind leg, because the muscles, tendons and ligaments are scattered over a greater length of bone. In any position that you may place a *low* hock, a horse will have greater difficulty in moving his hind foot forward to a point equal to the track made by the forefoot. Thus, he is forced to reduce his stride and his ability to travel with the greatest maximum use of his muscular power.

I have often heard "so-called" smart horsemen say that they want a hock low to the ground because a breed of dogs known as greyhounds have low hocks and it is said that this contributes to their ability to run. This argument is nothing short of gross ignorance and should be ignored by any right thinking horseman, due to the fact that a dog can flex his spine forward from his pelvis bone toward his shoulders, thereby increasing the reach of his hind legs. A horse cannot flex his spine from his pelvis bone toward his shoulders and to compare the anatomy and position of the hind leg of a horse to that of a dog is ridiculous as is proven in the following drawing. Furthermore, the anatomy of a greyhound is not constructed so as to carry any weight on his back.

HIGH HOCKS

Racing men and those who use speed horses, as well as breeders of horses for fancy carriage and draft purposes, sometimes will be caught making the remark that they favor a *high* hock. As in the case of low hocks, we will assume that the distance from the ground to the top of the rump is the same. The only way to have a

31

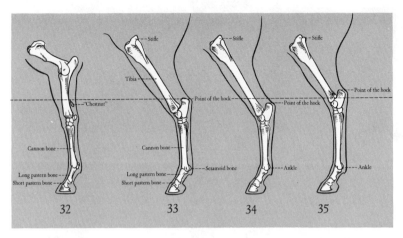

| *Inside foreleg* | *Ideal hock* | *Low hock* | *High hock* |

high hock is to *shorten* the tibia bone from the stifle to the hock and *lengthen* the cannon bone from the ankle to the point of the hock, which would give you a hock of *high* position as shown in Illustration 35. This hock causes the concentration of power of the muscular development from the hock to the stifle and increases the distance from the hock to the ground. This position draws the hock in under the body by reason of the short bone from the hock to the stifle. The short bone sets the leg forward. The long bone increases the reach, which causes this horse to be forced to cut his forelegs down at a rapid rate of speed, whether it is a fast trot or a run. This causes the horse to go unsound in front by the severe damage that will be done to his muscles, tendons, joints and feet of his forelegs by the toes of his hind legs.

Many horse shoers have been blamed and condemned for not being able to stop a horse from "cutting" and even milder cases of "forging," when it was not the horse shoer's fault at all. The fault was in the anatomy of the horse which could not be corrected by man-made mechanical devices and should have been blamed on an unbalanced hind leg with a *high* hock.

Nothing good can come from a sickled hock. The weight of the horse and the jar from the ground is all placed upon the articulating bones of the hock and would cause throughpins to develop which will eventually cause bog spavin. This same hock is susceptible to "curbs" forming on the back part of the hock by reason of the undue pressure and displacement of the small articulating bones of the hock. The front part or face of the hock is in such a cramped or unnatural position that injury to the small bones of the hock will cause the growth of bone spavins, either to the side or to the center of the hocks. This same sickled, overly curved hock does not lend the proper spring-like function to the tendons and also the growth of unnatural bone structure such as "curbs" and "spavins" will interfere with the movement of the joint and the movement of the tendons.

It is often said that a horse that "sets under" at the hocks has an "easier" stop. This is easily understood. First, before the hock goes unsound, the horse naturally favors the hock joints and is inclined to let his forefeet slip rather than to cause pain to these weak hocks. Then as this horse is put into hard use and malformations begin to cause undue pain, he will for sure favor the hock joints and slide his feet, reducing the shock to the rider. A horse stopping in this manner loses a great deal of power and puts stress and strain on the ankles, knees and shoulders in front, which will cause stiffness to develop in his forequarters. The side effects of unsoundness in any quarter of a horse must be borne by the relative parts of his anatomy and this always causes a burden and stiffness and unsoundness eventually in some other part of the horse's anatomy.

After having scaled out the legs of more than fifteen hundred horses for balance and soundness, and having taken into consideration that these horses had been used in performance sports and working jobs in which they had foregone much stress and strain, together with their age and present condition of soundness, I am convinced beyond all reasonable doubt that the following is true.

The proper balance between the height of the hock and the fore-leg can be arrived at by taking the distance from the ground to the top of the "chestnut" on the inside of the foreleg (which is the degenerated remains of the third toe of the pre-historic horse), as a point from which to measure. The two measurements taken from the topmost point of the "chestnut" to the ground between the forefeet and measuring from the point of the hock to the ground just below the ankle and just behind the foot, must be the same. This means that you could stretch a string from the top point of the "chestnut" to the point of the hock and should have a reasonably level line.

I would conclude in the argument of high and low hocks that this line should be used as the level. A measurement higher or lower than this would constitute a high or low hock, both of which are unbalanced, will contribute to unsoundness and will be detrimental to the horse in his efforts to perform those feats that he is called upon to do.

GOOD HOCKS

The foregoing statements leave us to discuss the position of a *good* hock that is neither "high," "low," "sickled" or otherwise deformed. The distance from the ground up to the point of the hock and the distance from the point of the hock up to the head of the tibia bone at the stifle should be exactly the same length. This is essential to good balance in the hind leg of a horse. The back point of the hock should be squared and well defined. The hock joint should stay in a straight line continuing down the back of the leg to the head of the cannon bone and should not set under to any degree. The front of the hock should be reasonably flat, with no meatiness or fatty appearance. A hock should be well chiseled and well defined. There are several reasons why a hock needs to have this construction. First, the tendons and ligaments produce a spring-line action that is necessary before the hock can propel the body of the horse forward or enable the horse to rear back and raise the forefeet off the ground. This square, rugged hock joint gives the tendons a strong spring-like action. The tendon on this hock will be well away from and following a straight line down the cannon bone, which puts it in excellent position to go around the sesamoid bone at the back point of the ankle as shown in Illustration 33. This would reduce severe pressure on the sesamoid bone as the tendon goes on down to the pastern. This well defined, pointed hock greatly facilitates the spring-like function of the tendons and reduces the possibilities of string halter, bowed tendons and other forms of injury that tendons may be exposed to.

A straight hock has far greater closing and opening leverage, which adds to the ability of the horse's leg to reach forward and adds to the ability of the leg to travel backwards, because there is no binding between the main bone of the tibia and the bone of the cannon which would cause displacement of the six small articulating bones of the hock. A straight hock beginning a forward motion from the point of the toe has only to drive the body forward from a straight line to the ground to the top of the hock. A hock with any degree of "set" causes the movement to make a circular pattern before the hock can drive the horse forward.

Feet

THE FOOT OF THE HORSE is the final determining factor in the horse's ability to perform and stay sound. Through the ages men have made sage remarks such as, "No foot, no horse." This saying is so old that I am sure no one could lay claim to having originated it. Books can be written about the feet, much of which is too technical to be understood by most readers other than the writers of such books.

The points of interest to the average horseman concerning the horse's feet can be easily covered by a description of the exterior appearance of the feet. A good foot should stand with a forty-five to fifty degree angle to the ground. It should always be large enough to carry the burden above it, endure the concussion caused by the movement of the horse, and be of hard and durable enough substance to resist wear from its constant contact with the various forms of the surface of the earth, from the softest of mud to rocks of many kinds.

The walls of the hoof consist of millions of fibers which are cemented together by the horny-like substance that is secreted from beneath the coronary band that encircles the top surface of the foot. The thicker and darker the walls of a hoof, the more serviceable they are to the horse. The sole of a horse's foot should be concaved, which is further proof that the wall of the foot was intended to carry the principal part of the weight.

The union of the wall and sole is generally evidenced by a small, white ring of welding substance formed from the bottom part of the foot to seal the sole in place. The wall of the hoof turns around the heel and inward from each side, forming a V-shape in the bottom of the hoof, which is referred to as the *bars* of the hoof. This incomplete circle is so designed that the hoof can expand and stand concussion.

The "frog" of the hoof is a soft, horny mass, lying in a V-shape, bordered on either side by the bars, and pointing out into the center of the sole of the foot. There is also an extension of fiber forming a band coming upward from the heel and around the top of the foot. If a foot were loose and disected, the frog would remain attached to the band aforementioned, and is not a part of the sole. At every step that a horse takes, pressure should bear on the frog. This pressure forms a pumplike action against a large blood vessel in the horse's hoof and forces blood to the outermost regions of the interior of the foot. This pumping action is also the reason that blood does not stagnate in the lower extremities of the foot and has its uplike flow back into the arteries to the heart.

Much could be written about the frog and when we got through writing it, it all could be covered by one statement: "Leave the frog alone." Horsemen and horse shoers are always trimming and cutting frogs and making them pretty. A continued paring and removing of the frog will result in a contraction of the hoof at the heel, which is the beginning of ringbones, sidebones and most all hoof malformations that are perpetrated on the horse by unskilled horsemen and horse shoers.

When examining a horse's feet, be sure that his forefeet are mates. The feet of horses often vary in shape and in their angulation to the ground. A horse with a stiltlike, perpendicular foot may also have a flat walled, shelly foot. Such mismatched feet are a problem to the horse in his efforts to perform and are a problem to those who are responsible for keeping the horse's feet sound. The forefeet of the horse are rounder and, in most instances, somewhat larger than the back feet.

The back feet of the horse should have the same general conformation. However, it is common for the back feet to be slightly smaller than the front feet, and somewhat more pointed at the toe, neither of which is considered a fault in the formation of the back feet. Back feet generally stand a little more perpendicular to the front feet, and this is not a fault in that the sharper toe and straighter foot aid the horse in his sudden movement from the ground.

Good feet are easier kept and will remain sound longer if a horse is not burdened with too much excess weight and is allowed to run free, instead of standing in a stall with shoes on. Many lamenesses have been cured by old horsemen simply by removing the shoes and turning the horse out to pasture on soft ground. In severe cases, even sand is better since at every step the horse puts pressure on the frog and the bars and forces the heels of the foot outward. All of this restores the natural circulation and general conformation of the foot.

Ponies have a shorter, more perpendicular foot than the large breeds of horses, and for the most part their feet are naturally sounder. However, ponies become lame from stall feeding and the lack of exercise quicker than the larger breeds of domestic horses. Too much feed and bodily care is an enemy of the feet of all horses.

The best feet are black in color. Dark amber or striped feet are ofttimes hard; but pure white horn on a foot is a bad fault because the lack of pigmentation reduces the hardness of the wall and the foot will not withstand the wear of hard surfaces. Neither does this light, soft horn hold the nails of a shoe as well as darker feet. There has always been a fad among people for stocking-legged, white-footed horses. And there have been many excellent horses that had white feet. But, from my way of thinking, they were good horses in spite of the fact that they had white feet; and, so far as I personally am concerned, the white foot never contributed anything to the betterment of a horse. I have often wished that all the white on horses was *put back in the barrel.*

Last, but not least, when the size of a horse's feet is in question, ninety percent of the time the wiser selection will be the larger-footed horse.

Irregular Pattern of Bone Structure

THROUGH THE AGES good horsemen have constantly endeavored to improve the different types of horses. These continuous efforts to improve horses so that they are more useful for some specific purpose such as draft horses, coach and harness horses, saddle horses, racing horses and so on, has caused the various breeds of horses to become distinctly different in size, body and muscular development and in the quantity of bone structure. Most breeders have pursued the special development of the body and muscular characteristics and seemed to have taken for granted that the *bone pattern* would follow in proportion to the other changes they have endeavored to make in their horses.

The cross-bred horse which contained a favorable combination of crosses has always been the most useful and has contributed more to the general economy of mankind than the various specialized breeds. It has been a common but seldom admitted practice that heavier boned pure bred horses or heavier boned cross-bred horses have often been bred into the breeds that had *lost* too much bone in the process of producing refinement and quality. Many times heavy boned horses of a certain breed have been crossed to lighter boned horses of the same breed with the intention of imparting more bone to the offspring.

May it be stated here and now that a great amount of *bone* and *substance* is seldom accompanied by *refinement;* and it may be equally stated that seldom do you find *refinement* and *quality* accompanied by an *abundance of bone substance.* This being true, breeders who seek to improve their horses have constantly cross-

47

bred bone structure of different quality and quantity in an effort to have framework to sustain an animal of performance and contribute to his endurance.

Some of the common remarks among horsemen are, "Look at that knee, what a good bone the horse has"; or "Look at that cannon, what a fine bone the horse has"; or "Look what a big, stout hock the horse has." Another great mistake and most commonly stated among horsemen: "Look what a fine head the horse has" and numerous other remarks that have been made by horsemen through the ages as they observe one part of conformation in the horse.

After having measured more than twenty thousand horses (I think nearer twenty-five thousand) I believe that I have discovered a fallacy in the cross-breeding of bone types that I have never before seen mentioned in my research of horse literature which has been written during the past several hundred years. This fallacy might well account for a large percent of the unsoundness, especially in the joint structure, of our modern horses which have been developed by cross-breeding. I have proven to myself beyond all reasonable doubt that the crossing of heavy boned and light boned horses does not by necessity *fix any pattern* of bone structure to be inherited by the offspring. The offspring, it is generally assumed, will have a compromise larger than the fine-boned parent and smaller than the large-boned parent. This assumption by breeders, in many cases, does not occur. *I am convinced that the bone structure is not necessarily what it should be in size as compared to the bone next to it.*

If both the sire and dam are of equal breeding quite often there will be a *nick* of the genes and the reproduced offspring would have an ideal blend of bone structure and the bone fibers would be of a continuous pattern. In the crossing of an extremely hot-blooded sire or dam to a cold-blooded sire or dam, a large percent of the offspring will be dominated by the hot-blooded side of the cross and very little compromise between bone structure will be accomplished. There will still be, from these same crosses, misfit bone patterns as well as other misfit conformation which is in part

48

the price we pay for the few good horses produced by cross-breeding. (In the statement of cross-breeding hot- and cold-blooded sires and dams, I do not mean to imply that well bred heavy boned horses are cold-blooded. The term "cold-blood" is meant to apply to horses that, themselves, are of several different crosses and do not possess dominant genes that would mark their offspring.)

A continuous pattern of sound and properly graduated bone structure in the skeleton of a horse is absolutely essential if the horse is to bear weight, endure stress and strain under adversity and remain sound and no worse off from his trials. I have found thousands of horses whose bone structure and joint formation was without conformity of pattern and with no uniformity of graduation as to the stress and strain to be endured. For example, a 12 inch knee should have an 8 inch cannon underneath it and not less than a 10½ inch ankle, the arm bone and muscling above the knee not to be less than 21 inches.

One of the worst variations from this graduation of good bone structure that I have ever found was in the case of a good, sound quarter type mare that had been crossed to a good individual of the Arabian breed. The offspring had an Arabian forearm of 17 inches, a quarter type knee of 13½ inches, an Arabian cannon of 7¾ inches and an Arabian ankle of 9¼ inches. This knee, by comparison, would resemble trying to attach a 5½ inch pipe (at the position of the knee) to a 3¾ inch pipe without the use of a reducer or bushing. A knee and cannon with this much extreme in size would have such an unbalanced fitting that the leg from the knee down may either be crooked to the outside or to the inside because of the lack of properly fitted cannon bone at the base of the knee as shown in Illustration 37.

The pattern of bone structure does not necessarily change above or below a joint. The lack of *nick* could very easily occur in the smaller bones of the knee which would contribute greatly to *popped knees* or other unsoundness of knee joint structure because the stress, strain and concussion from the ground, and the body of the horse would not be properly cushioned by the uneven bone structure of the knee, as shown in Illustration 39.

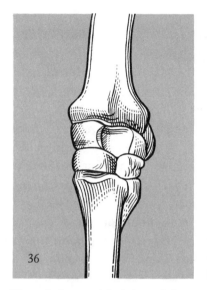
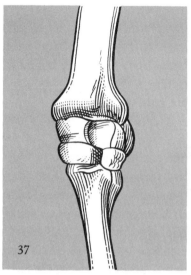

Normal knee with balanced bone structure.

Knee with extremely small cannon bone which would have an unbalanced fitting and from the knee down is crooked to the outside.

The 9¼ inch ankle of the aforementioned horse would not carry the weight of a cross-bred animal's body or bear the strain of concussion if this horse had been put to any useful service, and the muscling of the forearm would not be equal to the task of lifting such an unbalanced leg and moving it forward for any reasonable length of time under stress.

This same horse had a 15½ inch hock which would have been sufficient to withstand the stress and strain of an Arabian size body but not the weight of a cross-bred horse's body and is severely under the necessary 17½ inch measurement to have been in proportion to his knee (the knee being 13½ inches and belonging to a quarter type horse). He had a 9¼ inch back cannon bone which could have handled the weight of the cross-bred body but was out of proportion to the 15½ inch hock above it and the union in the joint between two bone structures of this much difference (as shown in Illustration 41) will not remain sound under the stress and strain required of it to propel the body forward. The back

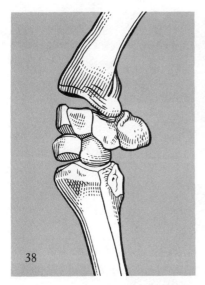

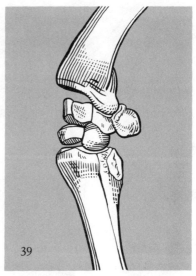

Normal knee showing well balanced articulating "rocker" bones of the knee joint that will withstand concussion.

Abnormal knee shows proper sized arm bone above and proper sized cannon bone below but with small "rocker" bones insufficient in size and strength to withstand concussion. This type of knee is often referred to as a "calf-knee."

ankle measurement of 10½ inches which the horse had is composed of the base of an extremely large cannon bone resting upon a normal size pastern bone as shown in Illustration 43.

In summary, this horse has inherited two bone measurements from his dam (knee and back cannon) and four bone measurements from his sire (front cannon, front and back ankles and hock) that are apparent to the naked eye. We cannot accurately determine the variances of the bone structure that are covered by flesh, however, these measurements are conclusive proof that this cross did not produce a *nick* and a uniform cross-bred horse was not produced. I have found thousands of horses that had either one bone or one joint that did not fit the rest of the bone structure of their body. All of these horses were not necessarily cross-bred but certainly there had been no uniformity of bone pattern in their

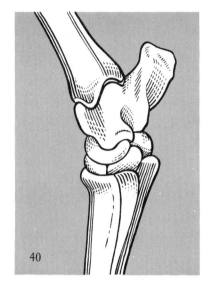
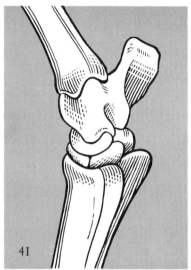

Normal hock with balanced bone structure.	*Abnormal hock with extremely large cannon bone and poor union of same.*

This uneven position will displace the articulating small bones that form the hock joint and would tend to increase the incidents of bog spavin, curbed hocks, etc. This type of hock often appears to be "capped" when actually it is a malformation of the hock joint. It might be noted further here that it is difficult for a joint to set in proper position under a horse when its proportions are not right.

sires and dams and it should not be assumed by breeders that when crossing bone sizes they are going to get a compromise in size all the way through the bone structure of the offspring.

Much of the bone structure of a horse's frame is not visible to the naked eye but with knowledge and practice a great deal of that can be estimated by feeling of the spine at the tail set and examining the skull structure where the head is attached to the front vertebra of the neck which is known as the Atlas vertebra. Other unsoundness occurs in the case of stifle injuries and pelvis fractures which are caused by excessively good muscling of the hindquarters that is covering a very weak stifle or pelvis bone structure.

It is not my intention to discourage the cross-breeding of horses. I have long contended that careful cross-breeding produces hybrid

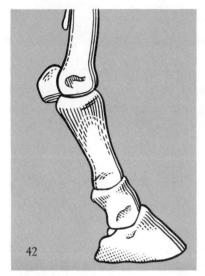 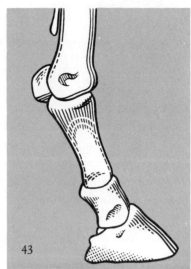

Normal ankle and cannon.   *Ankle with improper sized cannon bone.*

The ill-fitting position of the large cannon bone forming the upper part of the back ankle will reduce the leverage of the ankle and pastern, increase the strain on the sesamoid and add to the tendency of stumbling and breaking over from behind.

vigor and greatly improves temperament and disposition in the offspring. It is my purpose to point out the many disappointments and failures to be experienced in cross-breeding and to further emphasize that only the few outstanding individuals produced by the proper *nick* should be considered for future breeding purposes. It may well be said that promiscuous and unplanned cross-breeding can be blamed for the thousands of misfit horses of poor conformation, etc.

Will He Carry Weight?

THE PRESENT-DAY HORSEMAN seldom gives much thought or attention to a horse's ability to carry weight other than in the circles of handicapping in reference to race horses. The factors contributing to a horse's ability to carry a good amount of weight need to receive more attention in our selection of breeding and using horses.

Since weight rests upon a horse's back, let's give due consideration to the conformation of the region of the back where the weight is going to be placed. A horse's back should be well arched over the loin, and the coupling should be equal in height to the top point of the withers. The "rib spring" should start out from the spine almost perpendicular and carry well to the side before the taper of the ribs begins downward, as shown in Illustration 44. This shape of back provides a good foundation for the load of weight that is to be placed upon the horse whether it be in the form of a pack or a man. On a back of this type the weight will move the least possible amount backward, forward, or sideways; which means he will not have to be cinched uncomfortably tight, and there will be a very minimum amount of damage or irritation caused to the surface of the back by a constant carrying of the load. A horse with this shape of back will be able to carry the greatest amount of weight with the least possible damage to his back and with a minimum amount of fatigue.

Since the earliest known pattern of Mongolian, Barb and Arabian primitive saddles, the bars of saddles trees have always been constructed to run parallel to the spine and to rest upon the "upper" spring of the ribs. This construction causes the weight to be evenly distributed across a greater area of the body and reduces the possibility of fatigue.

In the case of a sharp, narrow, "rafter-type" back with the rib spring starting an immediate downward angle from the spine, as shown in Illustration 45, the inside of the bars of the saddle tree will catch against the rib spring. The outside of the saddle bars

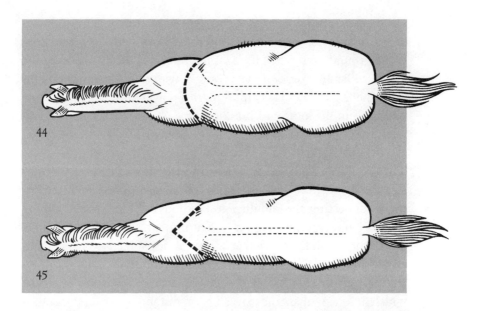

will not be making firm contact with the horse's rib spring, and the center of the saddle will be allowed to rest directly on the top of the spine. This uneven distribution of weight will cause back sores and "fretfullness," and the discomfort to the horse will be increased because the saddle will have to be tightly cinched to hold the weight in position.

Horses that are much lower at the withers than at the coupling have greater difficulty enduring the weight of a rider or pack in that the load is constantly working forward, which creates a greater burden on the shoulders, knees, ankles and the muscling of the forelegs. In the case of pack-weights which are often used in the mountainous regions of North America, breeching harness and tail cruppers are more essential and cause more rubbing and chafing on a horse of low positioned withers. Another thing to be noted about a low withered horse carrying weight is the constant rubbing and chafing caused by the front cinch working too far up under the shoulder, all of which lessens the horse's serviceable ability to carry weight.

Horses with extremely high withers and low coupling experience more discomfort from carrying weight uphill because breast collars are essential and often interfere with free breathing due to the fact that a horse climbing a hill must work with his head closer to the ground than when he is on level ground thereby causing the breast collar to exert undue pressure against his windpipe. This type of horse usually lacks hindquarter power, also, and will show weakness in his loins and hindquarters.

SHOULDERS

The shoulder of a horse is attached to the thorax (body) by muscle, cartilage, sinew and the skin. There is no bone joint attachment connecting the shoulder to the body. A long, deep, sloping shoulder has a greater region of bearing surface against the body of the horse, and the burden of weight is distributed over the greatest possible area thereby lessening the possibility of acute strain on any part of the shoulder and allowing a free movement of stride, which is essential to the covering of distance. In comparison, a short shoulder has less bearing surface against the body and in order to bear the equivalent weight that a long shoulder would bear, the muscling and cartilage must become more rigid and fibrous, reducing the maneuverability of the shoulder and causing a premature stiffness to develop because of this thickening of the muscle fibers. The stiffening effect of this type of shoulder greatly hampers a horse's stride and lessens his ability to cover distance.

We have discussed the various types of horse's backs and shoulders where weight is to be placed, and it is simple to understand that the type of back and shoulders will determine to a great extent the amount of weight a horse can carry. The distance a horse can carry the weight and the time that would be required to cover that distance is largely dependent on the conformation of the shoulders, forearms, legs and girth.

FOREARM

The forearm of a horse that is muscled proportionately as well on the inside as the outside, and those muscles inside being firmly attached to the floor of the body, as shown in Illustration 46, causes the weight to be better borne by the foreleg and keeps the body

56

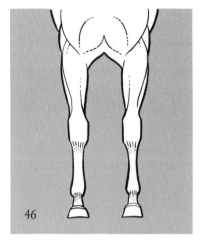 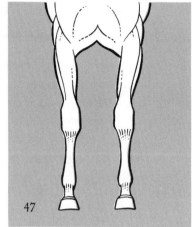

from a degree of "sagging" from the burden of top weight and contributes greatly to the staying qualities of a horse. A flat, weak-muscled inside forearm does not furnish sufficient support to the floor of a horse's body, as shown in Illustration 47, and causes a greater strain to be thrown on the muscling which attaches the body to the top of the shoulder which contributes to the incidents of muscular deterioration, commonly known as "sweeney."

LEGS

Regardless of the conformation of the weight-carrying region of a horse's body, he must be properly balanced in the muscling ratio between the forelegs and the backlegs, and he must have sound-ness of joints and correct position of bone structure.

GIRTH

The final determining factor of a horse's weight-carrying ability and endurance is the conformation of his body through the girth, the region that houses the heart and lungs, which must be deep from the top of the withers to what is commonly referred to as the floor of the body (where the cinch goes under the horse) which should be wide and flat.

In summary, it may well be said that a horse's ability to carry weight cannot exceed his conformation and soundness.

The Top Line

HORSEMEN HAVE THEIR DIFFERENT LIKES AND DISLIKES that they conclude as they approach a horse and since this generation has not lived horseback as much as those who have gone before, much has been forgotten about the value of the *top line* of a horse.

Most all light-boned horses from 14.2 to 15.2 hands high are about seven feet long from the poll of their head between their ears to the cheek of their rump. The way this seven feet is divided on top can tell you a lot about where the shoulders, hindquarters and legs of your horse are positioned.

In Figure 48 you can see that this neck is a little bit longer than the back—the length of the neck being considered from the poll between the ears to the point just below the forepart of the withers, and the length of the back being considered from the forepart of the withers to the coupling.

The withers are well mounted above the shoulders and will set the rider comfortably back of the forequarters and into the middle of the horse's back.

This back is reasonably short and in view of the fact that the neck is a little bit longer than the back, you will know that the shoulder is well sloped which assures you that the horse will have abundant stride of the forelegs since he can reach his foot out to a point equal to a line drawn from the slope of the shoulder to the ground.

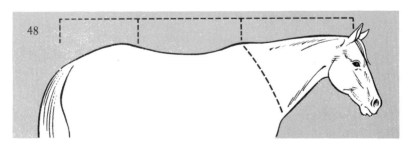

This illustration of a good top line shows the relative comparison of the length of the neck, back and rump.

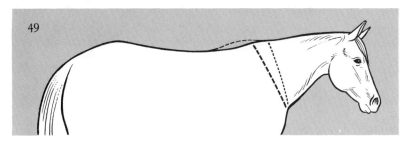

A short neck and a long back mean that this horse has lost stride and maneuverability of the forequarters as compared to the ideal top line.

This coupling, which is where the back and the pelvis bones come together, is slightly arched, well muscled and will give a firm feeling at any rate of speed. From the coupling to the cheek of the rump is as much or more than two-thirds the length of the back, which would indicate that the horse had a good hindquarter, is well stifled and would be capable of quick action and sprinter speed.

Now at a quick glance you have determined that the riding qualities of this horse would be comfortable and that he would have maneuverability of his forequarters and sufficient power in his hindquarters; the length and arch of this neck would indicate that this horse has a flexible poll and a good mouth.

You can see at a quick glance that the horse in Illustration 49 has a short neck and a long back with a reasonably good hindquarter. This means that the horse will have a straight shoulder, short stride, will be rough riding and it will be difficult to get a saddle to

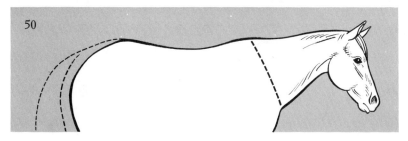

A short rump means that this horse has lost speed and power as compared to the ideal top line.

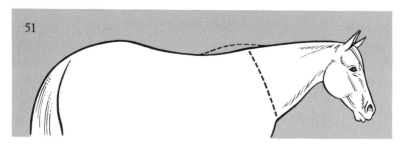

A low front means that this horse has lost balance as compared to the ideal top line.

fit his back that will not work forward and chafe at the cinch under the forearm. His ankles, knees and shoulders will stiffen and become unsound earlier in life because the rider is sitting directly over them.

This horse will also have lost some ability to flex his poll due to the shortness of his neck, which will give him inferior maneuverability and lessen his power to jump.

The neck and back of the *top line* shown in Illustration 50 are equal in length with a well-mounted wither and a sloping shoulder but with a decidedly short line from the coupling to the cheek of the rump. This horse will have the appearance of having an exceptionally good "front end" which in fact is not true. His "front end" is no better than it should be but the shortness of his hindquarters and the weakness of his stifle gives the optical illusion that his "front end" is tremendous.

A horse with this *top line* has lost sprinter speed and quick driv-

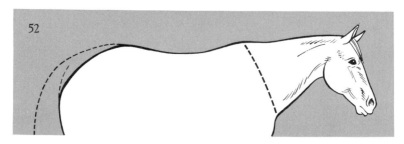

This horse has a "goose rump" and consequently has lost enduring speed, quickness and is more susceptible to injury as compared to the ideal top line.

ing action that is so necessary in any using type horse and will have a somewhat soft or weak feeling under the rider.

The *top line* shown in Illustration 51 tells you that this horse will carry you in the position of "riding downhill" at all speeds. The lack of balance prevents this horse from having the proper forward stride of his legs and he will be handicapped in most any useful purpose that you might need to put a horse to.

Needless to say it is hard to find saddles or riders that can stay put on a back like this.

Illustration 52 shows a *top line* of an otherwise good horse except that he is goose-rumped. This type of hindquarter is objectionable because the poor shape and development of the muscles rob this horse of enduring speed and lessen his quickness of leaving the ground.

It was also known when horses were used more severely that goose-rumped horses were more susceptible to injury at the coupling (causing bobbiness) and were easier stifled than properly muscled horses.

Quite often the joints of the hind leg of a goose-rumped horse are not in proper line with the joints of the foreleg.

Stride

IT IS COMMONLY CONCEDED AMONG HORSEMEN that a horse who can walk good is able to handle his feet and legs and will have balance at the other extended gaits such as the trot and gallop. It is a common remark among horsemen, "If he can't walk he can't do anything right."

The natural stride of a horse at a walk is generally considered to be normal and satisfactory when he picks his forefoot up and moves it forward a proper distance and his back foot is brought forward and placed in the track made by the forefoot at the last movement. This is considered good, normal walking stride as shown in Illustration 53.

53   54

*Good natural stride which is attained by careful selection in breeding to pro-
duce properly positioned legs.*

A good natural stride at a walk will propel the horse forward
the full length of his body from his withers to the cheek of his
rump. In order for a horse to have this satisfactory movement his
legs will have to be in position with the "four corners" of his body,
figuratively speaking, and when he is at a standing position his
hind legs will be in a position that a straight line could be drawn
from the cheek of the rump to the point of the hock to the back of
the ankle to the ground. His forelegs will be in a position that a
straight line drawn upward through the center of the ankle, the
center of the knee, the center of the elbow and through the shoulder will strike the forepoint of the wither (see Illustration 54).

Over-Reach is a term applied to the movement of a horse who
has the ability to pick his forefoot up in such a manner as to enable
his hind foot to be placed forward beyond the track made by the
forefoot. Over-reach in the stride of a horse is valuable to reduce
the shock to the rider and to cover ground more rapidly. The
greater the natural over-reach is the smoother the movement will
be and the greater the distance the horse can cover with a minimum amount of effort.

Over-reaching is desirable in a horse that we naturally term a
"daisy clipper," meaning that he barely lifts his forefeet high
enough to clear the earth or any obstacle thereon, such as rocks,
limbs, or uneven terrain, without exerting any unnecessary
amount of effort. In the event of any adversity this horse has saved

55	56

Poor stride by reason of training.   *Good style and action attained by careful selection in breeding.*

all the maneuverability of his forelegs and can cope with holes in the ground, stumps, rattlesnakes, etc. He can readily be jumped into motion, galloped, reined or called upon for any sudden handling action.

A riding horse with these qualities is very useful in the utility purposes of a horse and has a maximum amount of endurance because he does not exhaust himself by unnecessary leg work and covers the greatest possible amount of distance with the least possible effort.

The contrast or extreme of a horse with the above described movement is seen in Illustration 55. This horse is showing a terrific amount of so-called style, much of which has been obtained by extremely long feet, weighted shoes, leather soles and possibly lead under the soles of the shoes, and being trained with boots on and other weights such as chains fastened between the ankles and feet.

The time required for this horse to snap his knee high into the air prevents him from being able to extend the foreleg to the proper stride before it is necessary for him to pound the earth with that foot in order to snap the other knee into the air. This in effect means that he has lost the possibility of forward reach by the upward movement of the leg and has merely picked his foreleg up, waved it around in the air and put it back on the ground in a very short distance from where he picked it up and thereby has not obtained the proper distance in the stride of his foreleg.

Improperly positioned legs.   *Poor stride by reason of conformation.*

This horse apparently is producing a great stride with his hind legs and is over-reaching his front tracks an unbelievable distance of eighteen or twenty inches or even more and, by so doing, is reducing the shock to the rider. However, due to the fact that he did not cover a desirable distance with his foreleg movement because of his animated motion, the over-reach of the hind foot is misleading and in fact is "farcical."

This is one example of improper movement of the legs and poor stride. This horse would be at a loss to collect himself for a sudden movement to cope with bad terrain and obstacles or to be able to avert an accident which would depend upon the maneuverability of the legs. This horse's performance is artificial, man-made, impractical and is not necessarily the fault of the horse's conformation. Such so-called action that has been so artificially and brutally gained is certainly non-transmittable to an offspring and nothing has been achieved toward the breeding of a better horse by such methods.

This is not intended to make light of a horse having a desirable amount of style, symmetry and rhythm in his way of going that has been obtained by careful selection and breeding for desirable conformation (see Illustration 56).

Bad conformation reduces stride as shown by Illustration 57. A quick glance at this picture will show that the forefeet are placed on the ground far back behind a straight line drawn from the forepoint of the withers to the ground, and the hind feet are set way forward under the horse's body, further than a straight line from the cheek of the rump shows a good hind foot position to be. The distance between the forefeet and hind feet is considerably reduced by this position and when the forefoot is moved forward it cannot reach the distance that the normal stride would be if it were placed directly in a straight line under the forepoint of the withers. The curve of the hock reduces the leverage of the hock and makes it impossible for the hind leg to reach as far forward as one properly positioned (see Illustration 58).

Consequently the entire motion of stride is shortened, the jar to the rider is increased and the necessary leg work of traveling a given distance is greater than that of a horse with normal stride, which is more exhausting to the horse and reduces his endurance. The more frequent pounding of the knees, hocks and ankles of this horse will contribute to early unsoundness.

A horse of this conformation will have very poor traveling ability at a walk, trot or gallop and about the only good thing that could be said of him is that he is "gathered up" and capable of stopping, however, it seems very foolish to have "brakes without motion."

Conformation of Brood Mares

A BROOD MARE SHOULD BE DURABLE AND SOUND as previously described. However, there should be additional attention paid to the selection of mares for breeding purposes. The general description that is found in various horse literature pertaining to brood mares tell that a brood mare should be slender necked with a refined throatlatch and a feminine appearance in the head. This same sort of literature refers to brood mare's appearance saying that they need to be an outstanding individual in order to improve the breed by passing on their more desirable characteristics.

It is more than theory that mares mark their male offspring to a greater degree than does the sire. Wise horsemen in selecting a stallion give more credit to the female side of the pedigree and to the individual brood mare that is the dam of some particular individual stallion that is being considered for breeding purposes. In the pedigrees of desert-bred Arabian horses, the brood mare line is diagramed on the top side of the pedigree and the sire's side is the bottom part of the pedigree. This is exactly reverse to the English and American way of diagraming a pedigree.

The better qualities of brood mares have been written about since man began to breed horses. However, very little can be found pertaining to the undesirable characteristics of brood mares.

Undesirable Characteristics:

1. The fact is generally conceded that all females do not possess all female genes and an admixture of male genes can be observed in some mares. In examining the teeth of a mare, special note should be made in regard to the tush between the front teeth and the jaw teeth that only studs should have. When a mare is carrying such a tush, it is an indication of male's genes and coarseness will accompany such a mouth around the jaws, throatlatch, neck and general appearance of the head.

2. A mare with a heavy crested neck is likely to be hard to breed. An arched neck is very desirable, but a crested neck covered with coarse flesh and fat gives a masculine appearance and is another warning sign that such a mare will be hard to catch in season and harder still to cause her to conceive a foal.

3. Mares sometimes possess a very pronounced tailhead that sets up above the croup and is quite noticeable even to the unskilled eye. This sort of a tailhead is generally on the hindquarters of a mare that looks more male than female and is to be considered belonging to an individual that will be hard to breed.

The worst conformation defect that can be found on a mare does not necessarily belong to one that shows the presence of male genes. This is a mare who has pelvis bones that come forward from the spine and set at almost a triangle formation from the spine out to the hip joint. This malformation is not noticeable to the untrained eye and is referred to by the few that would know as a forward offset pelvis. Such a pelvis will never be flexible and causes such a mare to have extreme difficulty in delivering a live foal. If detected, they should never be kept as brood mares.

In selecting brood mares, care should be taken to choose mares with good balance in relation to the forequarters and hindquarters. Exercise extreme care in choosing the best of bone structure and soundness without thick shoulders and coarseness.

The Forward Seat

THE POSITION OF FORWARD SEAT RIDING *has stiffened more shoulders prematurely, bucked more knees and wind galled more ankles than any other misconceived riding practice of the last fifty years.*

I have listened in silence to the advocates of the forward seat for the last twenty years. I have seen and treated sore, stiff shoulders that had come to be that way apparently without cause. Knees have become less useful and more subject to breaking over, causing the horse to fall, without any apparent explanation. Ankles and pastern joints have taken an ever constant beating and produced wind galls on what otherwise might have been a durably sound horse.

This position of riding has been advocated by so-called horsemen who are literally without knowledge of the anatomy and mechanical functions of a good horse.

The position of a rider on a horse of good conformation and balance has long been known to be at the center of gravity or just behind the center of gravity toward the loins. This position of the rider has been easy to determine on a horse who possessed a well sloped shoulder, whose withers were set well back on his top line and whose back was short and strongly coupled at the loins. This type of horse, without being handicapped by some man-made contraptions called saddles, would naturally place the rider to the rear of the back point of the withers and just forward of the end of the loin muscles which means that the rider would be sitting at the "spring" of the horse's back. This position places the rider close to the origin of driving power that is derived from the spring and lever function of the hindquarters and loins of the horse. This position also places the rider back away from the direct line of the forelegs and shoulders. Consequently the rider receives less jar at this position than any other place that he can sit on the top of a horse. It is also true that the rider's weight is not pounding at a direct line over the shoulders, knees and ankles.

The position described above would be considered ideal to the rider for comfort and less damaging to the legs and body of the horse which by all logic and common sense would be the position that the horse could endure the longest and hardest use and would be the position that the rider could endure the longest ride over the roughest terrain or performance of the horse.

Now the forward seat in all its wrong mechanical position is this: The rider is placed over the shoulders in front of the center of gravity. His weight is constantly pounding the shoulders.

The shoulders of a horse are attached to the horse's body by ligaments, tendons, cartilage, muscle and skin and do not have a fixed connection with the "bone joint." The greater friction and more direct pounding that these shoulders must endure by the forward seat causes by necessity all the different tissue that holds the shoulders on the horse to become more fibrous and less elastic which results in the stiffening and soreness of the shoulders.

This same so-called modern forward seat causes the concussion of the weight to be greater on the forelegs and the pounding of the kneejoints to be much more severe, thereby causing the knee joint to have a tendency of "breaking over."

Since the same vibration, friction and jar hits the ankles it causes an excessive quantity of lubricating fluid to be produced by the lubricating glands of the ankle and especially the sesamoid bone which is a small spool mounted crossways at the back of the ankle. This excessive fluid is deposited in the tissues which produces what is known to the layman as "wind galls." Wind galls will never be found on a horse unless one of the following reasons exists.

First, a short pastern joint will cause a more direct pounding to the ankle.

Second, the improper shoeing and changing of the angle of the pounding to the ankle.

Third, the excessive forward weight caused to fall upon the ankle from a top line direction in the instance of the forward seat.

Now follow me carefully. A horse cannot clear the ground with both forefeet at the same time by the power of the forequarters. The only way that a horse can pick up both forefeet at the same time to produce a spinning action needed in working cattle, playing polo or to start the rhythm of a gallop is by the contraction of the muscles of the loins, the muscles of the hindquarters, the muscles of the stifles and gaskins and the bending of the hocks which enables the horse to lift the forepart of his body off the ground in what would be a modified rearing action. Now, with the forequarters lifted from the ground, the horse's ability to lunge forward or spin and turn is governed by the power of the hindquarters and the distance of the burden, which is the rider, from the seat of power, so the farther a rider sits up over the shoulders in the so-called forward seat the greater burden is placed on the hindquarters to handle this weight and the rider is causing the horse to suffer a "pinned to the ground" handicap by reason of his weight being so near the forequarters and so far from the muscles of the loins and hindquarters.

A line drawn from the center of gravity to the point of hoof of the hind leg is the line of thrust and the farther you remove the burden from the point of the hoof the longer you cause the line of thrust to be and the more power you lose from the hind legs.

I am used to all the common arguments such as jockies ride in a forward position. May I respectfully remind such advocates that if they will carefully study the pictures and drawings of a decade ago the jockies weren't sitting quite so much forward; and also may I point out that seventy percent or more of the injuries of racing horses are suffered in the mechanics of the forelegs and forequarters. May it be further stated that a jockey maintains racing position not more than two minutes and little regard could be given such arguments when durability and versatile soundness are the paramount objectives in the breeding of using type horses.

I sincerely hope that thinking horsemen will move back somewhat off the shoulders of their horses and not be ashamed of a saddle with a fifteen or sixteen inch tree that would better enable the rider to be in a comfortable position, both of which would contribute years of soundness to his mount.

How to Tell the True Age of a Horse by the Teeth

TO DETERMINE TRUE AGE OF HORSE STUDY:

1. Shedding of colt teeth to five years.
2. Cups in teeth to nine years old.
3. Shape and width of table of teeth from eighteen to twenty-three years.
4. Triangle of teeth from eighteen to twenty-three years.
5. Narrowness and width of teeth from twenty-four to twenty-nine years.

Always observe length of teeth together with the gum line and gourd seed of shaft of teeth.

HALF YEAR: *The outer and inner edges of nippers are worn, while only the outer edge of the middle teeth is worn, and the corner teeth have not yet come into contact.*

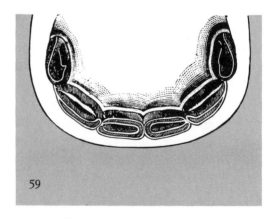

59

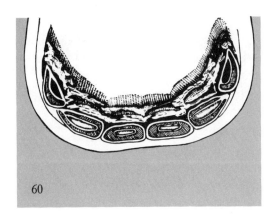

TWO YEARS: *Four middle nippers show wear and the inner edge of corner teeth show wear.*

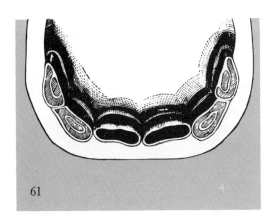

TWO AND ONE-HALF YEARS: *The horse nippers are just pushing through the gums, while the middle and corner teeth not shed (foal teeth) present a smooth, worn surface. Nippers will be full grown at three years old.*

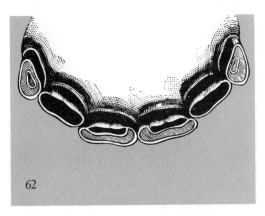

THREE AND ONE-HALF YEARS: *The second pair of horse nippers have come through and will begin to wear when the horse is four years old.*

FOUR AND ONE-HALF YEARS: *At four and a half years the foal teeth are all gone from the lower jaw. The nippers show wear on both edges, and the outer edge of middle teeth is worn. The hook teeth and corner teeth of the horse are just appearing. Until the corner teeth begin to wear horsemen will refer to this mouth as a "soft" five-year-old.*

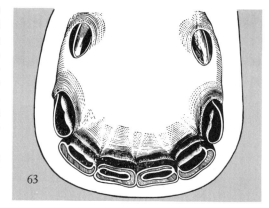

FIVE YEARS: *Now the horse has a "full mouth" which means that he has all permanent teeth. All teeth have "cups" in the center. The two middle teeth are worn until the cups are shaded—but not gone.*

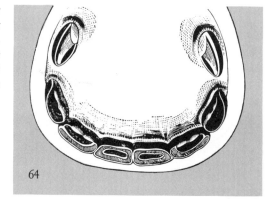

SIX YEARS: *The cups are worn from the two middle teeth and shaded in the next tooth on both sides of the middle teeth.*

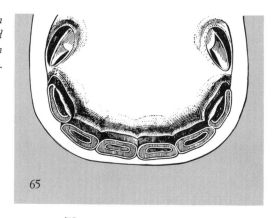

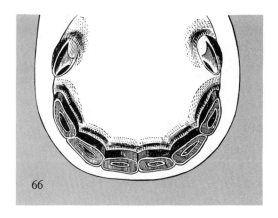

SEVEN YEARS: *The corner tooth has a well-defined cup; the outside corner of the next tooth has a small cup left. The hook teeth have begun to show wear.*

66

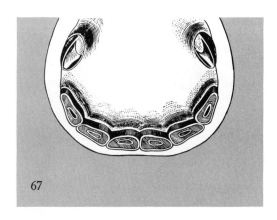

EIGHT YEARS: *The corner teeth have a cup left "open in the corners" as horsemen say. The "point" of the hook teeth have worn off. The inside corners of the middle teeth have begun to get thicker.*

67

68

NINE YEARS: *The upper corner teeth have a cup left, however, the corner teeth below are smooth. Horsemen would say, "barely smooth."*

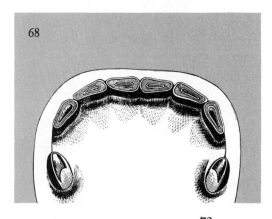

EXPLANATION:

Cups are black spots in teeth from three years to nine years. Shaft is length of entire tooth. Table is grinding surface of tooth.

TEN YEARS: *All four center nip-pers are getting thicker from front of teeth to inside.*

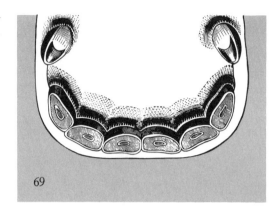

69

ELEVEN YEARS: *Upper nippers have gotten thicker. Inside cor-ner tooth is thicker too.*

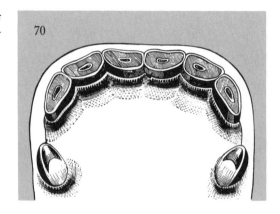

70

TWELVE YEARS: *Showing the lower jaw at twelve years old. The nippers are round or nearly so—as thick as they are broad. The second pair are get-ting round, and the corner teeth are gaining in thick-ness by comparison with their breadth.*

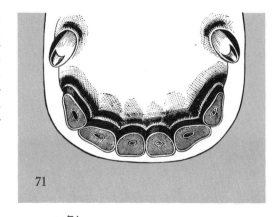

71

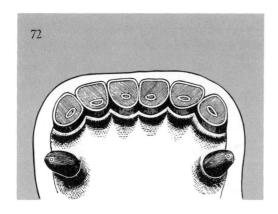

SEVENTEEN YEARS: *The corner teeth of the upper jaw become round at seventeen years old.*

Eighteen to twenty-three are the "triangle years." Beginning with the two center nippers the teeth start taking triangular shape at eighteen years old and at twenty-three years old all have taken a triangular shape table.

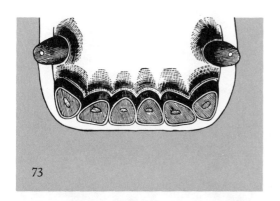

EIGHTEEN YEARS: *The nippers in the lower jaw are triangular at eighteen years old.*

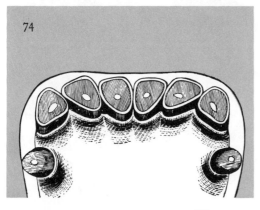

TWENTY-THREE YEARS: *The corner teeth of the upper jaw assume the triangular form at twenty-three years.*

Twenty-four to twenty-nine years are the years that the table of the teeth reverse and are twice as broad extending back into the mouth as they are wide from a front view.

TWENTY-FOUR YEARS: *The nippers of the lower jaw are now twice as thick as they are broad which is reverse position from seven years old (inset).*

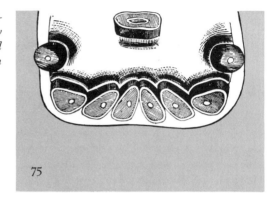

TWENTY-NINE YEARS: *The corner teeth of the upper jaw at twenty-nine years old are twice as thick as they are broad.*

SAND MOUTH: *This illustration shows a mouth that has been unduly worn by short grass in sandy pasture. The presence of cups in the corner teeth, shortness of the shaft and narrow white table of the teeth are all proof that this is a six-year-old horse with an eight-year-old mouth.*

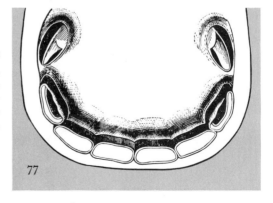

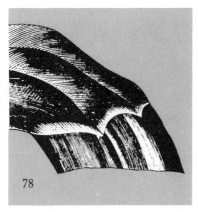

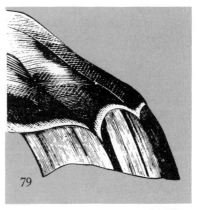

NINE YEARS: *The upper jaw at nine years old—a side view. Hook on corner tooth is further evidence of nine years old.*

TWELVE YEAR HOOK: *Will wear off by sixteen due to change in angulation.*

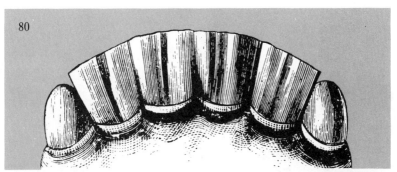

Five-year-old front view—study the "gum line," observe how straight the gum line crosses the tooth.

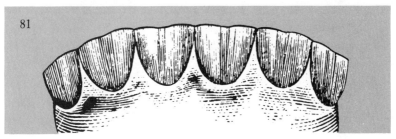

Twenty-year-old "gum line" has sagged far down through the years. Gum line of lower teeth is always true indicator of age.

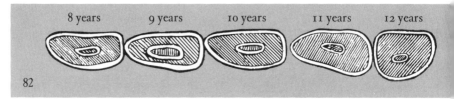

8 years   9 years   10 years   11 years   12 years

82

This illustration is composed of center nippers, beginning with eight years through seventeen years, that are placed in a row to show how much wider the table of the tooth has gotten in ten years.

The rough outside ridges running up and down the long way of the shaft of the tooth are referred to as "gourd seed." These ridges start forming on the middle teeth at ten years old and continue to form on other teeth working toward the corner teeth. The corner teeth are ridged or "gourd seeded" by fourteen to sixteen years old.

83

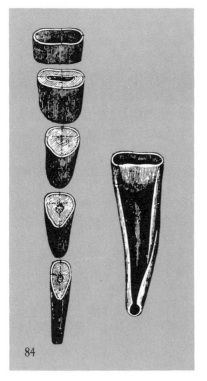

84

A tooth cut to show how table of tooth will appear at three years, six years, twelve years, eighteen years and twenty-four years old.

78

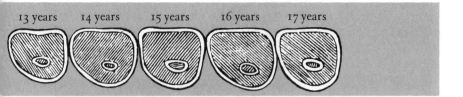

85

86

Outside view of the teeth of a six-year-old horse with the flesh removed to show the shaft of the tooth arched from the bone sockets to the table. Hook teeth show at side.

Inside view of the teeth of a six-year-old horse with the flesh removed to show the curve of the shaft of the teeth and how they are embedded into the jaw.

The study of these illustrations will clearly show that the teeth are embedded into the jaw which is not as wide as the mouth, causing the shafts of the teeth to be formed with different dimensions from the table of the three-year-old teeth to the bone sockets of the teeth. As the teeth are pushed out by bone and cartilage growth the table of the teeth change shape thereby giving an accurate index of age.

LONG TEETH: *Upper teeth in this illustration from top view of table would appear to be six years old.*

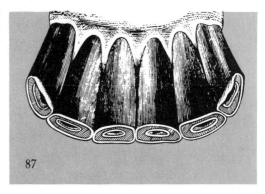

87

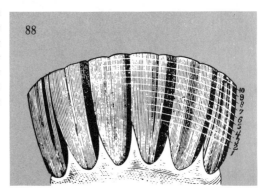

88

Lower front view shows ten years of extra growth lines which added together makes the horse sixteen years old. The table on long teeth will show the horse to be younger than his true age. The gum lines shows to be old.

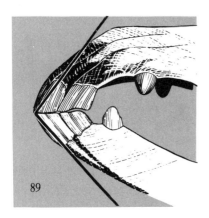

89

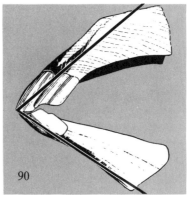

90

Ten-year-old that has some little more inclination than six-year-old.

The inclination in this twenty-year-old has greatly increased in ten years. The added slope further reduces the effectiveness of the teeth in chewing.